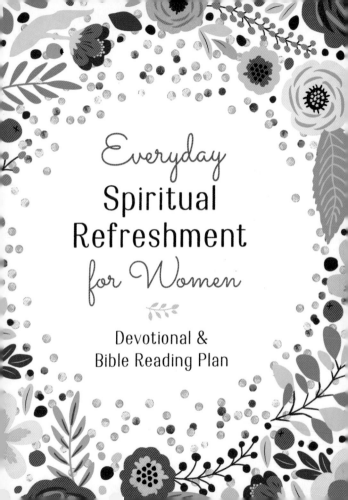

Everyday
Spiritual
Refreshment
for Women

Devotional &
Bible Reading Plan

Everyday
Spiritual
Refreshment
for Women

Devotional &
Bible Reading Plan

BARBOUR BOOKS
An Imprint of Barbour Publishing, Inc.

ISBN 978-1-64352-265-4

Published by Barbour Books, an imprint of Barbour Publishing, Inc., 1810 Barbour Drive, Uhrichsville, Ohio 44683, www.barbourbooks.com

Our mission is to inspire the world with the life-changing message of the Bible.

ecpa Member of the
Evangelical Christian
Publishers Association

Printed in China.

Introduction

Many people would like to read through the Bible in a year—but we know from personal experience, that can be a real challenge. That's why we created *Everyday Spiritual Refreshment for Women*—to give you the encouragement you need as you begin this life-changing journey.

In addition to daily scripture readings for every day of the year—an Old Testament, New Testament, and either Psalms or Proverbs passage—this book also features 365 challenging and encouraging devotional thoughts, each highlighting a particular Bible promise from that day's scripture selection.

Each day's Bible reading should take 15 to 30 minutes to complete. If you stay with it, you'll soon be able to say, "I read through the Bible in a year!"—and you'll undoubtedly find your life changed by the great promises of God's Word.

Day 1

Genesis 1–2; Matthew 1; Psalm 1

---

*On the seventh day God
had finished his work of creation,
so he rested from all His work.*

GENESIS 2:2 NLT

Many women put in forty hours a week at a full-time job and then come home to care for the house and family. Don't forget to take time out for yourself. If God rested after working all week, then it's important to take care of yourself. Press the pause button and rest your mind, body, and emotions. You're worth it. Take a moment and relax.

Day 2

Genesis 3–4; Matthew 2; Psalm 2

*When they saw the star,
they were overjoyed.*

MATTHEW 2:10 NIV

Can you imagine the wise men, gazing upon that star for the first time? Finally! The long-awaited day had come. What joy they must have felt in their hearts. Surely they could sense the beginning of a new era. The Gospel message is all about new beginnings. We rejoice every time we're given a chance to begin again. Praise God for the many times He's given you a fresh start.

Day 3

Genesis 5–7; Matthew 3; Psalm 3

But You, O Lord, are a covering around me, my shining-greatness, and the One Who lifts my head.

PSALM 3:3

You never know where courage will pop up in your life, because you never know what you'll face that will require it. You can be sure, though, that God will give you courage when you need it. God is both your Protector and your Strength. So be confident that whatever you face, you do not face it alone.

Day 4

Genesis 8–10; Matthew 4; Psalm 4

I will lie down and sleep in peace.
O Lord, You alone keep me safe.

PSALM 4:8

Your body was designed to perform like a battery. It runs down and has to be recharged. That's why sleep is so important. It's a time of restoration for your body and your mind. The Lord has promised you the blessing of peaceful sleep. You can relax and take comfort knowing He never sleeps but watches over you at all times.

Day 5

Genesis 11–13; Matthew 5:1–20; Psalm 5

---

*"You are the light of the world—like a city
on a hilltop that cannot be hidden."*

MATTHEW 5:14 NLT

God means you to be a light set where the world can see it clearly—not a hidden flame behind closed doors, with curtains drawn. Being a light isn't always easy—people see everything you do, and they don't always like it. Don't let the critics stop you. Your works were ordained to glorify God, not make people comfortable. Knowing that, are you ready to shine today?

Day 6

Genesis 14–16; Matthew 5:21–48; Psalm 6

*"But I tell you, love your enemies and
pray for those who persecute you."*

MATTHEW 5:44 NIV

Without God's strength, could any of us follow this
command of Jesus for more than a very brief time?
Consistently loving an enemy is a real challenge. If
you hurt from pain inflicted by another, you hardly
want to pray for her. But loving actions and prayer
can bring great peace between two people at odds
with each other.

Day 7

Genesis 17–18; Matthew 6:1–18; Psalm 7

---

*And forgive us our debts,
as we forgive our debtors.*

MATTHEW 6:12 KJV

Is it true that God only forgives us to the extent that we forgive others? That's what the scripture teaches! It's so important not to hold a grudge. It hurts you, and it hurts the one you're refusing to forgive. If you've been holding someone in unforgiveness, may today be the day when you let it go. There is incredible joy—both in forgiving and *being* forgiven.

Day 8

Genesis 19–20; Matthew 6:19–34; Psalm 8

---

*"Therefore do not worry about tomorrow,
for tomorrow will worry about itself.
Each day has enough trouble of its own."*

MATTHEW 6:34 NIV

You can look ahead and obsess about fears for the future or take life one day at a time and enjoy it. But you only live in today, not in the weeks, months, and years that may lie ahead. You can only change life in the moment you're in now. Since worry never improves the future and only hurts today, you'll benefit most from trusting in God and enjoying the spot where He's planted you for now.

Day 9

Genesis 21–23; Matthew 7:1–11; Psalm 9:1–8

I will praise you, LORD, with all my heart. . . .
I will sing praises to your name, O Most High.
PSALM 9:1–2 NLT

Your words of praise are precious to your heavenly Father. His Holy Spirit who lives within you carries them straight to His throne. Why are your praises so dear to Him? Because they are the free expression of your heart. You chose Him when you could have chosen so many others. Lift your voice to Him. It brings Him great joy.

Day 10

Genesis 24; Matthew 7:12–29; Psalm 9:9–20

The Lord also keeps safe those who suffer.
He is a safe place in times of trouble.

PSALM 9:9

The Psalms often speak of God as a Refuge. Whether you face something large, like oppression, or something much smaller, He wants you to turn to Him in troublous times. Size does not matter, but your trust in Jesus does. Nothing you face is a shock to Him— He knows your troubles and has not deserted you. So go to your Refuge and take strength from Him.

Day 11

Genesis 25–26; Matthew 8:1-17;
Psalm 10:1-11

Why standest thou afar off, O Lord?
why hidest thou thyself in times of trouble?

PSALM 10:1 KJV

Have you ever felt like God was unreachable? Like He was deliberately hiding when you were in trouble? It's interesting to realize that God is usually not the One who's moving. You are. If you're feeling far from God today, take a step in His direction. And if you've been really far away, may this be the day you choose to run into His arms.

Day 12

Genesis 27:1–28:9; Matthew 8:18–34;
Psalm 10:12–18

---

*O Lord, You have heard the prayers of those
who have no pride. You will give strength to
their heart, and You will listen to them.*

PSALM 10:17

It's easy to feel unheard in this life. Even your closest friends may sometimes fail to listen. But God hears. He's never too tired, too busy, too distracted. You don't need an appointment. So cry out to Him. Share everything with Him. Let Him in on your secrets and your hopes. He will never fail you.

Day 13

Genesis 28:10–29:35; Matthew 9; Psalm 11

While Jesus was having dinner at Matthew's house, many tax collectors and sinners came and ate with him and his disciples.

MATTHEW 9:10 NIV

Christian women often shy away from those who don't share their faith, but Jesus didn't. In fact, He reached out to the most unlikely, unlovable people. Today, as you face people in your world who don't yet know the Lord, begin to view them as Jesus viewed them. . .as people in need of loving. Then ask your heavenly Father what you can do to play a role in leading them to Him.

Day 14

Genesis 30:1–31:21; Matthew 10:1–15; Psalm 12

When Rachel saw that she had not given birth to any children for Jacob, she became jealous of her sister. She said to Jacob, "Give me children, or else I am going to die!"

GENESIS 30:1

Jealousy is such a problem among women, isn't it? Even Christian women can be envious of one another. Today, take inventory. If you find yourself wishing you had the latest, greatest house, car, outfit, gadget, or gizmo just because your friends have those things, release those desires to the Lord. He owns it all, anyway. Replace your jealousy with thankfulness for the things you already have and the blessings the Lord has poured out.

Day 15

Genesis 31:22–32:21; Matthew 10:16–36;
Psalm 13

How long wilt thou forget me, O Lᴏʀᴅ?
for ever? how long wilt thou
hide thy face from me?

Psᴀʟᴍ 13:1 ᴋᴊᴠ

Women love to be nurtured. We love to feel
secure. Sometimes when we've been praying for
something for a long time without a clear answer
from the Lord, we feel He's abandoned us. That He
doesn't care. There's good news today, daughter of
God! He will never leave you or forsake you. He's
right there, waiting for you to crawl up in His lap.
Why not take some time right now to do just that?

Day 16

Genesis 32:22–34:31; Matthew 10:37–11:6;
Psalm 14

---

*"He who wants to keep his life will have it
taken away from him. He who loses his life
because of Me will have it given back to him."*
MATTHEW 10:39

Have you ever clung too tightly to something? The
Lord wants us to have a loose grip on both material
possessions and our very lives. He's the owner. The
manufacturer. And He's the One with the how-to
manual. God has your life completely under control. So don't cling too tightly. . .to possessions,
attitudes, or thought patterns. Have a loose grip on
things and a tight grip on the Lord.

Day 17

Genesis 35–36; Matthew 11:7–24; Psalm 15

God said to him, "Your name is Jacob, but you will no longer be called Jacob; your name will be Israel." So he named him Israel.

GENESIS 35:10 NIV

As a little girl, did you practice writing your "married" name every time you had a crush on a boy? When you gave your heart to the Lord, He gave you several new names—daughter, bride, and princess. . .to name a few. You are His and He is yours! Today, celebrate the fact that everything about you has changed. . .right down to your name!

Day 18

Genesis 37–38; Matthew 11:25–30; Psalm 16

You will show me the way of life. Being with You is to be full of joy. In Your right hand there is happiness forever.

PSALM 16:11

When we stay on God's path—His road—we experience fullness in every area. And if we stick close to Him, which we are called to do, we will experience joy—not just now, in this life, but forevermore. Can you imagine. . .a joy that never ends? Draw near to the Lord. In His presence you will find fullness of joy.

Day 19

Genesis 39–40; Matthew 12:1–29; Psalm 17

---

*"And his name will be the hope
of all the world."*

MATTHEW 12:21 NLT

Are you faithful to pray for other believers around the globe? Women in every country need your prayer support. Today, before you set off on your way to influence your own world (your family, neighborhood, workplace), spend a little time thinking about—and praying for—women in countries to your north, south, east, and west. May the whole world come to know Him!

Day 20

Genesis 41; Matthew 12:30–50; Psalm 18:1–15

The Lord is my rock, and my safe place,
and the One Who takes me out of trouble.
My God is my rock, in Whom I am safe.
He is my safe-covering, my saving
strength, and my strong tower.

PSALM 18:2

Some women seem to be as solid as a rock! They hold together when the kids are upset, don't lose their cool when the plumbing needs repair, and manage to hold their tongues when coworkers and friends are having a bad day. What about you? Feeling invincible? If not, don't fret! You don't have to be rock solid. Instead, look to God. . .your Rock, your foundation.

Day 21

Genesis 42–43; Matthew 13:1–9; Psalm 18:16–29

Joseph then ordered his servants to fill the men's sacks with grain, but he also gave secret instructions to return each brother's payment at the top of his sack. He also gave them supplies for their journey home.

GENESIS 42:25 NLT

Joseph was a man who understood pain and betrayal. After all, he'd been abandoned by his own brothers and even sold off into slavery. But, when the opportunity came to repay evil with evil, how did he respond? Joseph blessed his brothers with all they needed and more. He repaid evil with good. Today, as you face people who've treated you badly, make a choice to bless.

Day 22

Genesis 44–45; Matthew 13:10–23;
Psalm 18:30–50

*"This is why I speak to them in picture-
stories. They have eyes but they do not see.
They have ears but they do not hear
and they do not understand."*

MATTHEW 13:13

Have you ever searched for something, only to
discover it was right in front of you? Sometimes
we don't see the obvious. The same is true in
our relationship with the Lord. Sometimes He
attempts to speak to us—through His Word or
circumstances—and we simply don't see or hear.
Today, press in close and ask for His understanding.

Day 23

Genesis 46:1–47:26; Matthew 13:24–43;
Psalm 19

The heavens declare the glory of God;
and the firmament sheweth his handywork.

PSALM 19:1 KJV

Look outside right now; better yet, go outside. Just look around you. If you live in a concrete jungle, look up at the sky. Imagine for a moment the immensity of God's creation, the grandeur of it. And yet, He calls mankind His most splendid creation. God values you above all else. Look up at the sky and consider that.

Day 24

Genesis 47:27–49:28; Matthew 13:44–58;
Psalm 20

---

*"The holy nation of heaven is like a box of
riches buried in a field. A man found it and
then hid it again. In his joy he goes and
sells all that he has and buys that field."*

MATTHEW 13:44

Have you ever stumbled across a rare treasure—
one so priceless that you would be willing to trade
everything you own to have it? If you've given your
heart to Christ, if you've accepted His work on Cal-
vary, then you have already obtained the greatest
treasure of all: new life in Him. Oh, what immea-
surable joy comes from knowing He's placed that
treasure in your heart for all eternity!

Day 25

Genesis 49:29–Exodus 1; Matthew 14; Psalm 21

The king shall joy in thy strength,
O LORD; and in thy salvation
how greatly shall he rejoice!

PSALM 21:1 KJV

It's so important to pray for our leaders. They need our daily intercession for their safety and wisdom. Today, as you contemplate your current political leaders, pause a minute and lift their names up in prayer. May they all find strength in the joy of the Lord. May each come to the fullness of salvation. And may the people rejoice as a result of what the Lord has done!

Day 26

Exodus 2–3; Matthew 15:1–28; Psalm 22:1–21

"I promise to bring you out of the suffering of Egypt to the land of the Canaanite, the Hittite, the Amorite, the Perizzite, the Hivite, and the Jebusite, to a land flowing with milk and honey."

EXODUS 3:17

Lord, how amazing heaven must be. As much as we try to be of the world and not in the world, we are bombarded with foul language, violence, addiction. We are a people who so much want to change others. We want them to be strong, faithful, kind, like Jesus. How I look forward to the heaven You've prepared for Your followers—a land without sin.

Day 27

Exodus 4:1–5:21; Matthew 15:29–16:12;
Psalm 22:22–31

---

*Our children will also serve him.
Future generations will hear about
the wonders of the Lord.*

PSALM 22:30 NLT

When we plant seeds in our children, we're really planting them in their children and their children's children. It really puts things in perspective. Today, as you pass on nuggets of truth to your children, imagine the impact you're having on generations to come. How many lives will be changed because you took the time to teach your children the things of God?

Day 28

"Then I will take you for My people, and I will be your God. And you will know that I am the Lord your God. I will bring you out from under the heavy loads of the Egyptians."

EXODUS 6:7

God freed the Hebrews from slavery and brought them to their new land. But He didn't stop there. Today He still proves Himself to people by freeing them from sin's slavery and creating loving relationships with them. Has God freed you from sin? Then know Him intimately. Draw near and enjoy His blessings, no matter what "slavery" you've faced before.

Day 29

Exodus 7:25–9:35; Matthew 17:1–9; Psalm 24

So Pharaoh's heart was hard and he would not let the Israelites go, just as the LORD had said through Moses.

EXODUS 9:35 NIV

Most women love transformation. Perhaps that's why makeover TV is so popular. We love to watch people and even things—rooms, houses, cars— change! Unfortunately, transformation isn't always so easy in the real world. Perhaps someone you know is in need of a spiritual makeover and you've been trying to get her to change. Today, acknowledge that only God can make over a heart. So leave it to Him!

Day 30

Exodus 10–11; Matthew 17:10–27; Psalm 25

He leads those without pride into what is right, and teaches them His way.

PSALM 25:9

You're known by the company you keep—even when it's God you're spending time with. As you read His words in the Bible and talk to Him about all the issues of your life, you cannot help but take on some of His characteristics. He is peace, and you become more peaceful. He is good, and you take on His goodness. It's all about the company you keep.

Day 31

Exodus 12; Matthew 18:1–20; Psalm 26

For where two or three are gathered together in my name, there am I in the midst of them.

MATTHEW 18:20 KJV

God loves to be where His people are. His Holy Spirit dwells in each one of them, but when believers come near each other, something heavenly happens—not only does He dwell in them, but He also fills the distance between them. In this atmosphere, the impossible becomes possible and love becomes manifest. God urges you to meet together with other believers regularly. He knows what can happen when you do.

Day 32

Exodus 13–14; Matthew 18:21–35; Psalm 27

Then Peter came to Jesus and said, "Lord, how many times may my brother sin against me and I forgive him, up to seven times?" Jesus said to him, "I tell you, not seven times but seventy times seven!"

MATTHEW 18:21–22

It's easy to want to give up on people who repeatedly hurt you and then ask for forgiveness. If someone has repetitively hurt you, ask the Lord to give you wisdom regarding the relationship, and then ask Him to give you the capacity to forgive, even when it seems impossible. Surely joy will rise up in your soul as you watch God at work.

Day 33

Exodus 15–16; Matthew 19:1–15; Psalm 28

---

*"You have led with loving-kindness the people
You have made free. You have led them in
Your strength to Your holy place."*

Exodus 15:13

By following Jesus, you always head in the right direction. Though the way may seem dark or convoluted, and you may often wonder if you're on the right track, as His Spirit leads you, you cannot go wrong. Your powerful Lord directs you in His everlasting way. If you start to go wrong, He will guide your steps. God's love never deserts His obedient child.

Day 34

Exodus 17–19; Matthew 19:16–30; Psalm 29

---

*But many that are first shall be last;
and the last shall be first.*

MATTHEW 19:30 KJV

Ever feel like you're at the bottom of the barrel? Like others get the cream on top of the coffee and you get the grounds at the bottom? Today, imagine things from God's perspective. He blesses at appropriate times and withholds blessing at others. Perhaps you're in a waiting season. Maybe there's a lesson to be learned from your current circumstances. Just remember, if you're last today, you could be first tomorrow!

Day 35

Exodus 20–21; Matthew 20:1–19; Psalm 30

For His anger lasts only a short time.
But His favor is for life. Crying may last for
a night, but joy comes with the new day.

PSALM 30:5

Don't you love second chances? New beginnings? If only we could go back and redo some of our past mistakes. . .what better choices we'd make the second time around. Life in Jesus is all about the rebirth experience—the opportunity to start over. Each day is a new day, in fact. And, praise God! The sorrows and trials of yesterday are behind us. With each new morning, joy dawns!

Day 36

Exodus 22–23; Matthew 20:20–34; Psalm 31:1–8

You have not given me into the hand of those who hate me. You have set my feet in a large place.

PSALM 31:8

Ever spent a significant amount of time in a really small space. . .say, an attic or a closet? After a while, you begin to feel closed in, like you're not getting air. Quickly you yearn for a large space! A wide-open field. A vast ocean. Confines are thrown off, and you're free to be all God created you to be. Today, may the Lord set you—and your thinking—in a large place!

Day 37

Exodus 24–25; Matthew 21:1–27; Psalm 31:9–18

Then Moses disappeared into the cloud as he climbed higher up the mountain. He remained on the mountain forty days and forty nights.

Exodus 24:18 NLT

Can you imagine following Moses into God's holy presence on that mountain? Enveloped by a heavenly cloud, distractions would surely fade away and you would be free to worship. . .truly worship. Today, the Lord stands at the door of your heart and knocks. Answer His invitation to come into His presence. Let your daily distractions—laundry, bills, conflicts, anxieties—fade as you spend time in that holy place.

Day 38

Exodus 26–27; Matthew 21:28–46;
Psalm 31:19–24

---

*Be of good courage, and he shall strengthen
your heart, all ye that hope in the LORD.*

PSALM 31:24 KJV

Hope is not some weak, airy-fairy kind of thing. It takes strength to put your trust in God when life batters your heart and soul. Weaklings rarely hold on to positive expectation for long, because it takes too much from them. But the spiritually strong put their trust in God and let Him lift up their hearts in hope. Then battering may come, but it cannot destroy them.

Day 39

Exodus 28; Matthew 22; Psalm 32

Be glad in the LORD, and rejoice,
ye righteous: and shout for joy,
all ye that are upright in heart.

PSALM 32:11 KJV

Have you ever been so happy that you just felt like shouting? Ever been so overcome with joy that you wanted to holler your praise from the rooftops for all to hear? Well, what's holding you back? Go for it! Shout for joy! Let the whole world hear your praises to the King of kings!

Day 40

Exodus 29; Matthew 23:1–36; Psalm 33:1–12

---

*"The person who thinks he is important will
find out how little he is worth. The person
who is not trying to honor himself
will be made important."*

MATTHEW 23:12

Oh, what a competitive world we live in. Everywhere you look, people are vying for position. What about you? Struggling to prove yourself? Concerned about your self-worth? Rest easy, daughter of God! You are a child of the King. Your worth is found in God alone, not your own accomplishments. Today He longs for you to find your value, not in what you've done, but in Him.

Day 41

Exodus 30–31; Matthew 23:37–24:28;
Psalm 33:13–22

_"This Good News about the holy nation of
God must be preached over all the earth.
It must be told to all nations and
then the end will come."_

MATTHEW 24:14

What do you think about Matthew's Gospel saying to go "over all the earth" and preach the Gospel? Ever feel like you're not doing your part? God calls us to be witnesses where we are—to bloom where we're planted. So instead of fretting over not doing enough, look for opportunities to share His message, and delight in the fact that you are usable. . . right where you are.

Day 42

Exodus 32–33; Matthew 24:29–51; Psalm 34:1–7

I will bless the LORD at all times: his praise shall continually be in my mouth.

PSALM 34:1 KJV

Praise the Lord. . .at all times? When I'm struggling with my boss? When the kids are fighting? When things aren't going my way? When I'm facing devastating losses or unexpected trials? Yes, even in the hardest of times, the Lord wants you to know that you can praise your way through them. Lift up your heart—and your voice. May the praises of the Lord *always* be in your mouth.

Day 43

Exodus 34:1–35:29; Matthew 25:1–13;
Psalm 34:8–22

---

*The LORD hears his people when they call
to him for help. He rescues them
from all their troubles.*

PSALM 34:17 NLT

As God's child, you have His ear 24-7, if only you will pray. Every need, trouble, or praise is His concern. And not only will He hear about your trials, He will deliver you from them. Feel discouraged in your troubles? You need not stay that way. Just spend time with Jesus. His help is on the way.

Day 44

Exodus 35:30–37:29; Matthew 25:14–30;
Psalm 35:1–8

*"His owner said to him, 'You have done well.
You are a good and faithful servant. You have
been faithful over a few things. I will put many
things in your care. Come and share my joy.'"*

MATTHEW 25:21

When you think of standing before the Lord—face-
to-face—are you overwhelmed with fear or awe-
struck with great joy? What a glorious day it will be
when we hear Him speak those words, *"You have
done well. You are a good and faithful servant."*
When He ushers us into the joy of His presence for
all eternity, our fears and hesitations will be forever
washed away.

Day 45

Exodus 38–39; Matthew 25:31–46;
Psalm 35:9–17

---

*My soul shall be joyful in the LORD:
it shall rejoice in his salvation.*

PSALM 35:9 KJV

Do you remember what it felt like to put your trust in Christ for the first time? You've probably never experienced anything else that brought such joy, such release: the overwhelming realization that the God of the universe loves you—enough to send His only Son to die on a cross so that you could have eternal life. There's no greater joy than the joy of salvation.

Day 46

Exodus 40; Matthew 26:1-35; Psalm 35:18-28

Let them call out for joy and be glad,
who want to see the right thing done for me.
Let them always say, "May the Lord
be honored. He is pleased when all
is going well for His servant."

PSALM 35:27

Do you ever feel like God's favorite child? Ever marvel at the fact that He continues to bestow His extraordinary favor upon you, even when you don't deserve it? God takes great pleasure in you and wants to bless you above all you could ask or think. So, when you're in a season of favor, praise Him. Shout for joy and be glad! Tell others about the great things the Lord has done.

Day 47

Leviticus 1–3; Matthew 26:36–68; Psalm 36:1–6

*Your love, LORD, reaches to the heavens,
your faithfulness to the skies.*

PSALM 36:5 NIV

God won't abandon you. He won't walk away. His faithfulness reaches further than you can see or even imagine. It's difficult to take in that kind of faithfulness in a world full of disappointments. But if you can be still long enough to sense God's never-changing presence and His steadfast commitment to you, you can survive the disappointments of this life so much more bravely. His faithfulness never fails!

Day 48

Leviticus 4:1–5:13; Matthew 26:69–27:26;
Psalm 36:7–12

"When you become aware of your guilt in any of these ways, you must confess your sin."

LEVITICUS 5:5 NLT

Perhaps you've heard the old saying "Confession is good for the soul." It's true! When you carry around guilt, it weighs you down. Today, if you're feeling the heaviness of guilt, take an active step to lay it down. Confess your sin to the Lord—and watch the weight lift. There! Doesn't that feel good?

Day 49

Leviticus 5:14–7:21; Matthew 27:27–50;
Psalm 37:1–6

*Delight thyself also in the LORD: and he shall
give thee the desires of thine heart.*

PSALM 37:4 KJV

What are the deepest desires of your heart? If you could really do—or have—what you longed for, what would that be? The key to receiving from the Lord is delighting in Him. Draw near. Spend time with your head against His shoulder, feeling His heartbeat. Ask that your requests come into alignment with His will. Then, with utmost joy, make your petitions known.

Day 50

Leviticus 7:22–8:36; Matthew 27:51–66;
Psalm 37:7–26

---

*Be still before the Lord and
wait patiently for him.*

Psalm 37:7 NIV

🌿

Do you remember waiting to open presents on your birthday as a child? "Just wait. It will all happen in due time," your mother would say. God sees the big picture, and He knows the right when, where, and how. So don't worry, just wait. You will see what God has promised you—all in due time.

Day 51

They went away from the grave in a hurry. They were afraid and yet had much joy. They ran to tell the news to His followers.

MATTHEW 28:8

Ever had a day where all of the news was good? You picked up the phone. . .good news. Read an email. . .good news. Then, the very next day, all of the news was bad! Even those closest to Jesus went through ups and downs. One moment they mourned His death. . .the next, celebrated His resurrection. Whether the news is good or bad—choose joy.

Day 52

Leviticus 11–12; Mark 1:1–28; Psalm 38

"Come, follow me," Jesus said, "and I will send you out to fish for people."

MARK 1:17 NIV

Have you ever been on a fishing trip? It's fun to bait your hook and cast your line. What anticipation! Will you get a nibble? Are you going to reel in "the big one"? Being a Christian is a bit like that. The Lord longs for us to bait our hooks—in the workplace, at the kids' swim practice, at lunch with a friend. So cast your line today! No telling who you might catch!

Day 53

Leviticus 13; Mark 1:29–39; Psalm 39

---

*I said, "I will watch my ways so I may not sin
with my tongue. I will keep my mouth
shut as if it were tied with ropes,
while the sinful are near me."*

PSALM 39:1

Life and death are in the tongue, and it's so easy to slip up and say the wrong thing, especially when emotions kick in. (C'mon, admit it! You know emotions can get the better of you sometimes!) Today, as you face challenges and situations, pay special attention to your tongue. "Watch your ways," as this scripture admonishes, and guard every word that tries to escape, especially the harsh ones.

Day 54

Leviticus 14; Mark 1:40–2:12; Psalm 40:1–8

*I waited patiently for the L*ORD *to help me, and he turned to me and heard my cry. He lifted me out of the pit of despair, out of the mud and the mire. He set my feet on solid ground and steadied me as I walked along.*

PSALM 40:1–2 NLT

When you've been living in the pit, you can hardly imagine being lifted out of it. Oh, the joy of knowing God can bring us out of even the deepest, darkest pit and place our feet on solid ground. Nothing is impossible with our Lord! If you're in a dark place today, call out to Him. . .and watch as He delivers you. He will establish your steps. Praise Him!

Day 55

Leviticus 15; Mark 2:13–3:35; Psalm 40:9–17

*I have not hidden what is right and good with
You in my heart. I have spoken about how
faithful You are and about Your saving power.
I have not hidden Your loving-kindness
and Your truth from the big meeting.*

PSALM 40:10

When you're a daughter of God, you have so much
to offer others. You're like a good book waiting to
be read. The pages are filled with stories of what the
Lord has done—how He's rescued you from sin, set
your feet in high places, and given you hope and
a future. Share your faith by sharing those stories
with others. You'll leave them begging for the next
chapter!

Day 56

Leviticus 16–17; Mark 4:1–20; Psalm 41:1–4

"He will make the holy place, and also the meeting tent which is in the center of the camp, clean and pure because all the sins of the people make them unclean."

LEVITICUS 16:16

Do you ever feel like you need to take a spiritual bath after hanging out with some people? Some folks think nothing of lying, cheating, or taking the Lord's name in vain. Maybe you've seen and heard too much. Your heart is heavy with a burden for coworkers or friends. Bring them before the Lord. Ask Him to do a purifying work in their hearts and lives.

Day 57

Leviticus 18–19; Mark 4:21–41; Psalm 41:5–13

And he arose, and rebuked the wind, and said unto the sea, Peace, be still. And the wind ceased, and there was a great calm.

MARK 4:39 KJV

Sometimes, Lord, I feel hopeless. I am so weak. I stumble. I cringe at the many sins I commit. Then, Lord, You remind me of Your disciples. Many were seasoned fishermen and, at sea, even they were afraid of storms. We are not worthy of Your grace, but our faith will lead us toward victory.

Day 58

Leviticus 20; Mark 5; Psalm 42–43

Then I will go to the altar of God, to God, my joy and my delight. I will praise you with the lyre, O God, my God.

PSALM 43:4 NIV

We're instructed to come into the Lord's presence with a joy-filled heart. . .to praise our way into the throne room. Perhaps you're not a musician. You don't own an instrument and only sing in the shower. Don't let that keep you from approaching the altar with a song of praise on your lips. Today, let joy lead the way, and may your praises be glorious!

Day 59

Leviticus 21–22; Mark 6:1–13; Psalm 44

Jesus said to them, "One who speaks for God is respected everywhere but in his own country and among his own family and in his own house."

MARK 6:4

It's strange to think that Jesus faced His toughest audience among His own people. But that's how it is for us sometimes too. Family members and coworkers can be harsh critics. And they don't always treat us with the respect we deserve. Maybe this is because we live in such close proximity or simply forget. Today, go out of your way to love those who are closest to you.

Day 60

Leviticus 23–24; Mark 6:14–29; Psalm 45:1–5

Beautiful words stir my heart. I will recite
a lovely poem about the king, for my tongue
is like the pen of a skillful poet.

PSALM 45:1 NLT

As a rule, we women love to talk. We're pretty good at opening up and sharing what's on our mind or in our heart, especially when we're happy. So what's in your heart today, daughter of God? Songs of praise? If so, don't be afraid to open up and let that joy spill over onto others. Let your tongue write the story. Let it flow!

Day 61

Leviticus 25; Mark 6:30–56; Psalm 45:6–12

---

*"Do not do wrong to one another,
but fear your God. I am the Lord your God."*

LEVITICUS 25:17

Sometimes we hurt others without even realizing it. When we use sarcasm, criticism, and unnecessary judgment, we bring pain to those we love. Sure, we might not be hurting the other person in an obvious sort of way, but it's likely our words carry a sting. Today, be on the lookout for the little ways you've been wronging others. . .and do an about-face!

Day 62

Leviticus 26; Mark 7; Psalm 45:13–17

A certain woman, whose young daughter had an unclean spirit, heard of him, and came and fell at his feet.

MARK 7:25 KJV

Perhaps you've been to the brink of desperation, at a point where you would do almost anything to see someone you love healed or delivered of an addiction, problem, or circumstance. Today, allow the desperation you're feeling to drive you to the Savior's feet. There, you will find the answers you seek and, ultimately, peace of mind.

Day 63

Leviticus 27; Mark 8; Psalm 46

God is our safe place and our strength.
He is always our help when we are in trouble.

PSALM 46:1

Have you ever gone through a trial or heartache so painful that you couldn't even put it into words? Any number of things could cause such suffering—loss, divorce, betrayal, sickness. If you find yourself in such a place, reach out to the Lord. He understands suffering at its deepest level. He knows how to comfort you. All you have to do is ask.

Day 64

Numbers 1–2; Mark 9:1–13; Psalm 47

Come, everyone! Clap your hands!
Shout to God with joyful praise!

PSALM 47:1 NLT

We women love a good party. Whether it's at a bridal shower, celebrating a new baby, or wishing someone a happy birthday, women love to have a great time. It's so easy to show our happiness to others, but what about God? When was the last time you shared your happiness with Him? Today, shout to the Lord with joyful praise. Celebrate His goodness!

Day 65

Numbers 3; Mark 9:14–50; Psalm 48:1–8

Jesus sat down and called the followers to Him. He said, "If anyone wants to be first, he must be last of all. He will be the one to care for all."

MARK 9:35

Do you want to be first? Ready your hands to serve. Be prepared to care for the needs of others before meeting your own. Sure, this flies in the face of what the world teaches. We live in a "me first!" generation, after all. But Jesus longs for us to humble ourselves and care for the needs of others. . . sacrificially.

Day 66

Numbers 4; Mark 10:1–34; Psalm 48:9–14

This God is our God for ever and ever:
he will be our guide even unto death.
PSALM 48:14 KJV

When we are facing dire troubles, God never deserts us. The Eternal One guides us every step of the way, whether life is joyous or discouraging. God never gives up on you and never fails you. So don't give up on yourself. When times are hard, hold on to Him more firmly. And in the end, you will step into His arms in heaven.

Day 67

Numbers 5:1–6:21; Mark 10:35–52; Psalm 49:1–9

No man can save his brother. No man can pay God enough to save him.

PSALM 49:7

If you're a typical woman, you may think you have superpowers. You can fix anything. Broken faucet? Stopped-up sink? No problem. But what about fixing people? Have you worked overtime and taken on the responsibility to save your friends and loved ones? While it's possible to be a seed planter, ultimately the salvation experience is between God and the individual. So fix what you can. . .and leave the rest to Him!

Day 68

Numbers 6:22–7:47; Mark 11; Psalm 49:10–20

"If anyone says to this mountain, 'Go, throw yourself into the sea,' and does not doubt in their heart but believes that what they say will happen, it will be done for them."

MARK 11:23 NIV

Don't you wish you had faith like this? Christians often try to gear up to it, willing it with all their hearts. But that's not what God had in mind. Manipulating Him cannot work.

Only when we fully trust in Him will He move our mountain—even if it's in an unexpected direction.

Day 69

Numbers 7:48–8:4; Mark 12:1–27; Psalm 50:1–15

When Moses entered the tent of meeting to speak with the Lord, he heard the voice speaking to him from between the two cherubim above the atonement cover on the ark of the covenant law. In this way the Lord spoke to him.

NUMBERS 7:89 NIV

We women have so many responsibilities that we often feel we're headed in several different directions at once. In the midst of the busyness, it's good to pause and spend time with God in a special "set aside" place. Choose a room in your home—or a quiet park or a backyard swing—and make that your "tent of meeting." Surely the Lord will speak to you there!

Day 70

Numbers 8:5–9:23; Mark 12:28–44;
Psalm 50:16–23

"A man should love Him with all his heart and with all his understanding. He should love Him with all his soul and with all his strength and love his neighbor as himself. This is more important than to bring animals to be burned on the altar or to give God other gifts on the altar in worship."

MARK 12:33

Not only are we to love others, we're to love them as we love *ourselves*. That's easier said than done! After all, some people are easy to love; others are not. But when we truly love God, He shows us how to reach out to the hardest of people. Make a special effort to love the unlovable. You'll be amazed at how God can melt even the coldest of hearts.

Day 71

Numbers 10–11; Mark 13:1–8; Psalm 51:1–9

And Moses said unto Hobab. . . , We are
journeying unto the place of which the LORD
said, I will give it you: come thou with us,
and we will do thee good: for the LORD
hath spoken good concerning Israel.

NUMBERS 10:29 KJV

There is nothing equal to a church home that feels safe, welcoming, constantly growing. Some churches are cold; some are scary; some are conservative; some are liberal; some. . . Well, the list goes on. Finding a good church home is just a tiny taste of what heaven must be like. All feel safe; all feel welcome; all can grow to be more like Him.

Day 72

Numbers 12–13; Mark 13:9–37; Psalm 51:10–19

Create in me a clean heart, O God;
and renew a right spirit within me.
PSALM 51:10 KJV

Your Creator delivers a masterpiece with every stroke of artistry He inspires. With each touch of His hand, with every letter you read in His Word, He changes your heart from old to new—forming you in His image. You become more like Him each moment you spend with Him. Your Creator makes all things new—and He's continually shaping the perfect you!

Day 73

Numbers 14; Mark 14:1–31; Psalm 52

I will give You thanks forever because of what You have done. And I will hope in Your name, for it is good to be where those who belong to You are.

PSALM 52:9

Women love to hang out with other women, particularly when they have things in common. And when women of God get together. . .watch out! There's an undeniable bond when Christian sisters unite. Today, praise the Lord for the godly friends He's put in your path. They're such a blessing, and they're not there by accident. The Lord has strategically brought you together. What a wonderful God we serve. . .together!

Day 74

Numbers 15; Mark 14:32–72; Psalm 53

"Watch and pray so that you will not fall into temptation. The spirit is willing, but the flesh is weak."

MARK 14:38 NIV

We've got to be on our guard for unexpected attacks. Temptation can strike at any point. We might feel strong—might convince ourselves we're not vulnerable—but our flesh is weak! We often end up giving in, even when we're determined not to. Today, ask the Lord to prepare you for any temptations that might come your way. Then, with joy in your heart, be on your guard!

Day 75

Numbers 16; Mark 15:1–32; Psalm 54

Pilate said to them again, "What do you want me to do with the Man you call the King of the Jews?"

MARK 15:12

Pilate asked the eternal question, "What do I do with Jesus?" We're confronted with the same question every day. What do we do with Jesus when we're facing trials? When we're struggling to get along with loved ones? When we're celebrating victories? Do we reach out to Him, lean on Him, look to Him for answers? Or do we forget He's there until desperation kicks in? What will you do with Jesus today?

Day 76

Numbers 17–18; Mark 15:33–47; Psalm 55

"Be sure to give to the LORD the best portions of the gifts given to you."

NUMBERS 18:29 NLT

Christians are called to give of their time, talents, and treasures. How can you give your time back to God? And what about your talents? Ask the Lord to show you how to use those to advance the kingdom. And your treasures? If you're struggling with giving to your local church, make this the day you release your hold on your finances. Give the Lord your very best.

Day 77

Numbers 19–20; Mark 16; Psalm 56:1–7

And Moses lifted up his hand, and with his rod he smote the rock twice: and the water came out abundantly, and the congregation drank, and their beasts also.

NUMBERS 20:11 KJV

Isn't it great how God makes provision at exactly the right time? He gives us just what we need when we need it. So why do we fret? Why do we wonder if He's going to come through for us? Hasn't He poured out blessing and provision time and time again? Ask Him for what you need, listen to His voice, then watch the water flow!

Day 78

Numbers 21:1–22:20; Luke 1:1–25; Psalm 56:8–13

The angel said to him, "Zacharias, do not be afraid. Your prayer has been heard. Your wife Elizabeth will give birth to a son. You are to name him John."

LUKE 1:13

Zacharias, though quite old, had been praying for a child for years. This answered prayer, though joyous, surely rocked Zacharias and Elizabeth's world! Have you ever consistently prayed for something without getting the answer you want? Ever felt like giving up? Don't! When you least expect it, your answer could come. . .and it might just rock your world!

Day 79

Numbers 22:21–23:30; Luke 1:26–56; Psalm 57

*"He has taken rulers down from their thrones.
He has put those who are in a place that is
not important to a place that is important.
He has filled those who are hungry with
good things. He has sent the rich
people away with nothing."*

LUKE 1:52–53

God provides for every one of His children, even the most humble. Wealth cannot gain His favor nor poverty destroy it. The Father does not look at the pocketbook, but at the heart. Those who love Him, though they may lack cash, will see their needs fulfilled, but unbelievers who own overflowing storehouses harvest empty hearts. God never ignores His children's needs. What has He given you today?

Day 80

Numbers 24–25; Luke 1:57–2:20; Psalm 58

And there were in the same country shepherds
abiding in the field, keeping watch
over their flock by night.

LUKE 2:8 KJV

Consider the shepherds in this verse. They were just doing their work, walking in daily obedience—nothing unusual at all. Then suddenly, the unexpected! God interrupted their "everydayness" with His master plan. What about you, daughter of God? Does your life feel a little humdrum at times? Well, get ready! If you're walking in obedience to the Lord, He might just interrupt your humdrumness with a life-changing adventure!

Day 81

Numbers 26:1–27:11; Luke 2:21–38; Psalm 59:1–8

O my God, take me away from those who hate me. Put me up high above those who rise up against me.

PSALM 59:1

Ever feel like the whole world's against you? Like people are out to get you? In this dog-eat-dog world, coworkers, neighbors, and even family members can be tough to deal with. So how do you respond when people lash out? Next time you're in that position, remember to turn to God first. Don't get mad. Just trust the Lord. He has the capability of raising you above your circumstances and even above your enemies.

Day 82

Numbers 27:12–29:11; Luke 2:39–52;
Psalm 59:9–17

---

*Then the Lord said to Moses, "Go up to this
mountain of Abarim, and see the land I
have given to the people of Israel."*

NUMBERS 27:12

Do you ever feel like you're wallowing in your circumstances? That you're in so deep you can't see the light at the end of the tunnel? Welcome to the fast-paced twenty-first century! Sometimes we need to climb above our troubles to see what God has for us. When we look at things from His perspective, we realize that hard times don't last forever. There's a great future ahead!

Day 83

Numbers 29:12–30:16; Luke 3; Psalm 60:1–5

John answered, "Anyone who has two shirts should share with the one who has none, and anyone who has food should do the same."

LUKE 3:11 NIV

Women are compassionate by nature. They love to give of themselves to others, particularly those in need. Today, take inventory of the people the Lord has placed in your path. Is there someone you should be reaching out to? Someone in need? Perhaps you don't have a lot to give. Maybe a smile or a kind word is all you have to offer. Regardless. . .give freely from a grateful heart.

Day 84

Numbers 31; Luke 4; Psalm 60:6–12

With God's help we will do mighty things,
for he will trample down our foes.

PSALM 60:12 NLT

We live in a self-sufficient day and age. We want to prove we can handle things on our own. However, the Lord doesn't want us to do anything without involving Him, particularly when we're confronted with tough challenges. He's here to help us. If you're facing a difficult situation today, remember that God is on your side. He's ready to go to battle for you. You are not alone!

Day 85

Numbers 32–33; Luke 5:1–16; Psalm 61

---

*From the end of the earth will I cry unto thee,
when my heart is overwhelmed: lead me
to the rock that is higher than I.*

PSALM 61:2 KJV

If you're like most women, there are some days when you feel invincible, and other days when you feel you're incapable of overcoming even the smallest of problems. Oh, but what a wonderful God we serve! When we are at our weakest, He is strong. He's bigger, higher, mightier, and greater than any problem we could face. And He's rock solid, never changing. Today. . .out of your weakness. . .call out to Him.

Day 86

Numbers 34–36; Luke 5:17–32; Psalm 62:1–6

---

*"I have not come to call good people. I have
come to call sinners to be sorry for their
sins and to turn from them."*

LUKE 5:32

Repentance isn't meant for "good people" who only
have "tiny" sins to confess. This verse reminds us that
no sin is too awful for God to hear about it. Each of
us may hesitate to confess sins and admit to wrongs
that embarrass us. But we are just the ones He calls.
One moment of repentance, and His Spirit cleanses
our lives.

Day 87

Deuteronomy 1:1–2:25; Luke 5:33–6:11;
Psalm 62:7–12

*"Why do you want to discourage the rest of
the people of Israel from going across to
the land the LORD has given them?"*

NUMBERS 32:7 NLT

Have you ever waited on the Lord for an answer
to prayer? Ever felt like one of the Israelites in
the desert—ready to quit before crossing the
Jordan into the Promised Land? God wants you to
persevere. Keep on keepin' on. Don't give up, and
don't allow the enemy to steal your godly desires.
Hang on! The Promised Land is coming! Dip your
toes in the Jordan today.

Day 88

Deuteronomy 2:26–4:14; Luke 6:12–35;
Psalm 63:1–5

---

*"Whoever hits you on one side of the
face, turn so he can hit the other side
also. Whoever takes your coat,
give him your shirt also."*

LUKE 6:29

Turning the other cheek goes against our human nature. More often than not, we want to fight back. As you face people who offend or hurt you, remember the words of Jesus from the verse above. His greatest desire is for you to live at peace with yourself. . .and fighting back is a real peace robber. Today, go out of your way. . .to turn the other cheek.

Day 89

Deuteronomy 4:15–5:22; Luke 6:36–49;
Psalm 63:6–11

*"Why do you look at the speck of sawdust in
your brother's eye and pay no attention
to the plank in your own eye?"*

LUKE 6:41 NIV

It's often easier to notice the flaws in others than to focus on their strengths. Why do we do this? Does it make us feel superior? Maybe it's because, like a red blob of paint ruining a fine portrait, flaws tend to stand out. They're easy to spot. Help us, Lord, to look past the stain and focus on the beauty—not only our own, but the beauty of others as well.

Day 90

Deuteronomy 5:23–7:26; Luke 7:1–17;
Psalm 64:1–5

*Love the LORD your God with all
your heart and with all your soul
and with all your strength.*

DEUTERONOMY 6:5 NIV

We talk about loving someone from the heart, but loving someone actually takes all of us. We don't just love God with our hearts. We love Him with our hearts, our souls, and our strength—we love Him with our whole selves. That's the kind of love He wants from you. You can lose your own self-focus in giving that kind of whole-self devotion, and losing your self-focus is what a surrendered life is all about.

Day 91

Deuteronomy 8-9; Luke 7:18-35; Psalm 64:6-10

The righteous shall be glad in the Lord,
and shall trust in him; and all the
upright in heart shall glory.

PSALM 64:10 KJV

Who do you run to when things go wrong? Most women run to their friends, their spouse, or their coworkers. But God wants you to know you can run to Him today. . .even with the toughest of problems. You are safe in your heavenly Father's arms. Make a conscious effort to cry out to the Lord before picking up the phone or sending an email. He's right there. . .waiting.

Day 92

Deuteronomy 10–11; Luke 7:36–8:3;
Psalm 65:1–8

---

*"So then, from now on, obey the Lord.
Do not be strong-willed any more."*

DEUTERONOMY 10:16

Are you a strong-willed woman? Like to get your way, even if it means pushing others aside to get it? This might be the norm among twenty-first-century women, but it's not what God wants. He longs for our hearts to be softened, for us to lay down our wills, our selfish ambition, and submit wholeheartedly to Him. Submission to our heavenly Father shapes us into strong, godly women.

Day 93

Deuteronomy 12–13; Luke 8:4–21; Psalm 65:9–13

"Those which fell among rocks are those who when they hear the Word receive it with joy. These have no root. For awhile they believe, but when they are tempted they give up."

LUKE 8:13

Imagine a sturdy oak tree, one that's been growing for decades. Its roots run deep. It's grounded. When the storms of life strike, that tree is going to stand strong. Now think of your own roots. Do they run deep? When temptations strike, will you stand strong? Dig into the Word. Receive it with joy. Let it be your foundation. Plant yourself and let your roots run deep.

Day 94

*All the earth shall worship thee, and shall sing
unto thee; they shall sing to thy name.*

PSALM 66:4 KJV

What is worship? Maybe the first thing that comes
to your mind is singing in a church service. The
truth is, worship comes in many different forms—
from the melody of a choir to a fevered revival
dance of a remote tribe in Africa. How can you
introduce a new way of worship into your daily
routine?

Day 95

Deuteronomy 16:9–18:22; Luke 8:40–56;
Psalm 66:8–15

---

*Many people were glad to see Jesus when
He got back. They were waiting for Him.*

LUKE 8:40

If you're like most women, you get a little impatient
sometimes. You don't like to wait. Maybe you're
even the same way when it comes to prayer. You
want your answer. . .and you want it now! Today,
turn your anticipation over to the One who knows
every answer and who longs to spend time with
you. Anticipate spending time with the King of
kings and Lord of lords!

Day 96

Deuteronomy 19:1–21:9; Luke 9:1–22;
Psalm 66:16–20

---

*Come and hear, all who fear God,
and I will tell you what He has done for me.*

PSALM 66:16

Everyone loves a great story, especially one with a happy ending. When you've given your heart to the Lord, you have the greatest story of all to tell. And when the Lord blesses you, which He so often does, that's just the icing on the cake. Don't be afraid to tell others what God has done in your life. People will be intrigued and even amazed. . .if you'll just open up and share.

Day 97

Deuteronomy 21:10–23:8; Luke 9:23–42;
Psalm 67

---

*Then Jesus said to them all, "If anyone wants
to follow Me, he must give up himself and his
own desires. He must take up his cross
everyday and follow Me."*

LUKE 9:23

What is your cross? What burdens do you bear? If
you're like most twenty-first-century women, you
want a carefree life, one without burdens. Jesus
understands firsthand that the Christian life is one
of sacrifice. There will be crosses to bear. Today, if
your desires have become your primary focus, lay
them down at His feet. Then, take up your cross. . .
and follow Him.

Day 98

Deuteronomy 23:9–25:19; Luke 9:43–62;
Psalm 68:1–6

But let the righteous be glad; let them rejoice before God: yea, let them exceedingly rejoice.

PSALM 68:3 KJV

Many women believe that happiness is a result of success. "I'll be happy when I find the right person to marry. . . . When I achieve my career goals. . ." The truth is that real happiness is the result of living in a right relationship with God. Regardless of what you may be facing—good and bad—be happy knowing you are pleasing your heavenly Father.

Day 99

Deuteronomy 26:1–28:14; Luke 10:1–20;
Psalm 68:7–14

"And the Lord today has made it known that you are His own people, as He promised you, and that you should keep all His Laws."

DEUTERONOMY 26:18

We so often look to our spouse, children, or friends, striving to feel accepted. Our Father already showers us with His love. How can we not acknowledge His promise? How can we not strive to keep His commands? We are treasured possessions!

Day 100

Deuteronomy 28:15–68; Luke 10:21–37;
Psalm 68:15–19

---

*"Everything has been given to Me by My
Father. No one knows the Son but the
Father. No one knows the Father but
the Son and the Son makes the Father
known to those He chooses."*

LUKE 10:22

Isn't it strange how some people are okay with talking about God but not Jesus? Some Christians play along because they don't want to ruffle feathers. But talking about Jesus—and His work on the cross—is absolutely unavoidable. He is the Way, the Truth, and the Life, after all! There's no other way to the Father but through Him. So speak the name. . .Jesus!

Day 101

Deuteronomy 29–30; Luke 10:38–11:23;
Psalm 68:20–27

---

*Our God is a God Who sets us free. The way
out of death belongs to God the Lord.*

PSALM 68:20

Ever feel trapped by your circumstances? Maybe you're struggling with an addiction that you can't overcome on your own. Perhaps you've hidden an internal struggle from those who know and love you. Today, as you spend time with the Lord, remember that He's a big God! He's a life giver, a chain breaker. Admit your weaknesses to Him and watch Him work to set you free.

Day 102

Deuteronomy 31:1–32:22; Luke 11:24–36;
Psalm 68:28–35

He is the Rock, his work is perfect: for all his ways are judgment: a God of truth and without iniquity, just and right is he.

DEUTERONOMY 32:4 KJV

Some people complain that God is unfair. But Moses, who suffered much for God's people, knew better than that. God is always perfect, faithful, and just.

We can have faith in God's perfection. He's never failed His people yet, though they have often been unfaithful. Trust in Him today. As He led His people to the Promised Land, He'll lead you home to Himself.

Day 103

Deuteronomy 32:23–33:29; Luke 11:37–54;
Psalm 69:1–9

---

*"May the one the Lord loves live by Him and
be safe. The Lord covers him all the day long.
And he lives between His shoulders."*

DEUTERONOMY 33:12

When you think of rest, you probably think of a
nap or soaking in a tub. While you need physical
rest, God wants your soul to be well rested as well.
Read encouraging scriptures that build your faith.
Spend time with Him in prayer. You'll feel like
you've had a spiritual power nap. You'll come away
rested and strengthened in your soul, safe from the
assaults of the day.

Day 104

Deuteronomy 34–Joshua 2; Luke 12:1–15;
Psalm 69:10–17

---

*"I say to you, My friends, do not be
afraid of those who kill the body
and then can do no more."*

Luke 12:4

Whom do you fear? If it's anyone other than God, take heart. You need not concern yourself with anything that person can do to you. Even those who can take your life can't change your eternal destination. So if someone doesn't like your faith, don't sweat it. Put your trust in God and serve Him faithfully, and you need not fear.

Day 105

Joshua 3:1–5:12; Luke 12:16–40; Psalm 69:18–28

[Jesus said,] Be ye therefore ready also:
for the Son of man cometh at an hour
when ye think not.

LUKE 12:40 KJV

Jesus promised His return, and He asked that His followers watch for Him. He hasn't told us when—only that it will be when the world least expects Him. Only those who are sensitive to His Spirit will recognize the times and the seasons. He expects you to live with the certainty that He will return soon. What a glorious day that will be. Look for it! Expect it!

Day 106

Joshua 5:13–7:26; Luke 12:41–48;
Psalm 69:29–36

*I will praise the name of God with song.
And I will give Him great honor
with much thanks.*

PSALM 69:30

It's one thing to spend time with God; it's another to praise Him with a thankful heart. Sometimes we forget His many blessings. We praise out of routine. Today, allow God to remind you of all the many ways He has blessed you. Oh, what full and thankful hearts we have, when we pause to remember! Now, watch your praises rise to the surface, like cream to the top of the pitcher.

Day 107

Joshua 8–9; Luke 12:49–59; Psalm 70

---

*"Do you think I came to bring peace on earth?
No, I tell you, but division."*

LUKE 12:51 NIV

There's nothing worse than division, especially when you care about the people involved. As women, we strive for unity. We're peacemakers. But Jesus prepared His followers for the idea that the Gospel can be a divisive message, particularly when unbelievers and believers dwell together. We can't control the thoughts or beliefs of others, but we can gauge our responses to them. Today, spend some time praying for those on the other side of the fence.

Day 108

Joshua 10:1–11:15; Luke 13:1–21; Psalm 71:1–6

Then the men of Gibeon sent word to Joshua at the tents at Gilgal, saying, "Do not leave your servants alone. Hurry and help us. For all the kings of the Amorites who live in the hill country have gathered against us."

JOSHUA 10:6

Though the Gibeonites had tricked Joshua into making peace with them, the Israelite leader held to his promise and went to the Gibeonites' aid when the Amorites attacked them.

Sometimes, like Joshua, we make imperfect promises. Will we faithfully fulfill them? Let's remember, God heard our words and holds us accountable.

Day 109

"Work hard to enter the narrow door to God's Kingdom, for many will try to enter but will fail."

LUKE 13:24 NLT

Many seek God but never find Him. That's usually because they're looking in the wrong place—they expect their own abilities to gain them heaven. They missed out on the fact that salvation doesn't depend on us: We cannot save ourselves through our own power. God's grace alone brings us new life and leads us through the narrow doors of eternity. Where are you looking for Him?

Day 110

"My brothers who went up with me made the heart of the people weak with fear. But I followed the Lord my God with all my heart."

JOSHUA 14:8

Caleb was a man who stood out from his fellow spies. While others brought fearful news to Israel, Caleb trusted God and encouraged them to seek the Promised Land. Near the end of his life, he maintained he'd followed God wholeheartedly.

Are we also wholehearted followers of our Lord? May fear or discouragement never keep us from walking in the path He prepares.

Day 111

Joshua 17:1–19:16; Luke 14:16–35; Psalm 71:22–24

My lips shall greatly rejoice when I sing unto thee; and my soul, which thou hast redeemed.

PSALM 71:23 KJV

Having trouble finding joy in your life today? Do what the psalmists often did and remind yourself what God has already done for you. How many ways has following Him blessed you? Begin by thanking Him for His saving grace, and the joy starts, no matter what you face today. Your lips will show the delight in your heart.

Day 112

Joshua 19:17–21:42; Luke 15:1–10; Psalm 72:1–11

"There will be more joy in heaven because of one sinner who is sorry for his sins and turns from them, than for ninety-nine people right with God who do not have sins to be sorry for."

LUKE 15:7

What a party heaven throws when one person comes to know the Lord! Can't you see it now? The angels let out a shout! The trumpeters play their victory chant. All of heaven reacts joyfully to the news. Oh, that we would respond with such joy to the news of a lost soul turning to the Lord. What a celebration!

Day 113

Joshua 21:43–22:34; Luke 15:11–32;
Psalm 72:12–20

"The father said to him, 'My son, you are with me all the time. All that I have is yours.'"

LUKE 15:31

Are you ever jealous of the attention that new Christians get? Maybe you've even noticed blessings in a new Christian's life that, to you, seem undeserved. God, like the father in the parable of the prodigal son, is gently reminding you that since you accepted His Son, all His blessings are yours. Embrace His love today!

Day 114

Joshua 23–24; Luke 16:1–18; Psalm 73:1–9

Choose you this day whom ye will serve. . .but as for me and my house, we will serve the Lord.

JOSHUA 24:15 KJV

From the mundane to the life altering, we make choices every day. Do you wish you could see into the future if you make this or that choice? Perhaps it's for the best that we don't have that option. But you can put your trust in the One who does. Listen to the Lord; choose Him. When you do, it will be much easier to make the right choices for your life.

Day 115

Judges 1–2; Luke 16:19–17:10; Psalm 73:10–20

"What if he sins against you seven times in one day? If he comes to you and says he is sorry and turns from his sin, forgive him."

LUKE 17:4

When another offends us, do we pass on the forgiveness we have received? That's what Jesus commanded. Remembering how gracious God has been to us, we need to show it to those who affront us too. As we think of our many sins that God put behind His back, can we fail to show compassion to others?

Day 116

Judges 3–4; Luke 17:11–37; Psalm 73:21–28

My flesh and my heart faileth: but God is the strength of my heart, and my portion for ever.

PSALM 73:26 KJV

We women need assurance—confirmation that we're pretty enough, smart enough, good enough. God wants you to know that "you are more than enough!" He is pleased with you. He wants you to be assured that He will always be there for you. You need not fear that He will grow tired of you, lose interest, or abandon you. You are precious to Him.

Day 117

Judges 5:1–6:24; Luke 18:1–17; Psalm 74:1–3

"But the man who gathered taxes stood a long way off. He would not even lift his eyes to heaven. But he hit himself on his chest and said, 'God, have pity on me! I am a sinner!' "

LUKE 18:13

Money isn't everything: the tax collector had learned the truth of that phrase. Without spiritual peace, his emptiness brought him low before God. But just then he'd come to the perfect place, for through his humility, God worked in his heart. The man went home from the temple justified. Do we also own humble hearts that are open to our Lord?

Day 118

Judges 6:25–7:25; Luke 18:18–43; Psalm 74:4–11

When Jesus heard this, He said to the leader of the people, "There is still one thing you need to do. Sell everything you have. Give the money to poor people. Then you will have riches in heaven. Come and follow Me."

LUKE 18:22

What do you own that keeps you from God? Nothing on earth is more worthy than heavenly treasure, yet earthly goods draw our hearts. We need to ask ourselves: What earthly possession could be better than our Lord? What could be worth giving up one moment with Him?

Day 119

Judges 8:1–9:23; Luke 19:1–28; Psalm 74:12–17

God is my King from long ago;
he brings salvation on the earth.

PSALM 74:12 NIV

The faith you hold dear is in the very same God as countless men and women throughout history. Think about it: fads come and go, technology emerges, governments rise and fall, even organized religion changes with the times. But your heavenly Father is the same God that held the heart of Hannah, Ruth, Elizabeth, and Mary Magdalene. Take comfort in His never-changing nature today!

Day 120

Judges 9:24–10:18; Luke 19:29–48;
Psalm 74:18–23

*Let those who suffer and those who
are in need praise Your name.*

PSALM 74:21

Do you feel you have to be on cloud nine to praise
God properly? That's not reality. Some of the best
praises come from oppressed and needy people who
cry out to God from their emptiness. Experiencing
His wonderful provision, they praise Him joyfully.

Ask yourself: What trouble has God allowed
you to experience so that you can open your lips
in praise?

Day 121

Judges 11:1–12:7; Luke 20:1–26; Psalm 75:1–7

For honor does not come from the east or the west or from the desert. But God is the One Who decides. He puts down one and brings respect to another.

<small>PSALM 75:6–7</small>

Sometimes we grumble when others are exalted. We feel left out. Why do others prosper when everything around us seems to be falling apart? God chooses who to exalt. . .and when. We can't pretend to know His thoughts. But we can submit to His will, and celebrate with those who are walking through seasons of great favor.

Day 122

Judges 12:8–14:20; Luke 20:27–47;
Psalm 75:8–10

*The children of Israel did evil again in the sight
of the LORD; and the LORD delivered them into
the hand of the Philistines forty years.*

JUDGES 13:1 KJV

Creeping sin slips into our lives, and we may not
want to recognize it. But God gently draws it to our
attention. If we don't respond, He'll persistently
remind us. If we stubbornly refuse to repent, He'll
eventually allow turmoil to enter our lives, as He
did with these children of Israel.

What does it take for God to get your attention?

Day 123

Judges 15–16; Luke 21:1–19; Psalm 76:1–7

"For they have put in a little of the money they had no need for. She is very poor and has put in all she had. She has put in what she needed for her own living."

Luke 21:4

Like this widow, could you give your last penny to God? Though her tiny coin wouldn't buy much, we're amazed when we read of this poor woman who gave so generously. Yet what is more secure than a gift given to God? What bank account or investment compares to Him? Her trust was all in Him—is yours?

Day 124

Judges 17–18; Luke 21:20–22:6; Psalm 76:8–12

*Every man did that which was
right in his own eyes.*

JUDGES 17:6 KJV

We've all seen an "I did it my way" attitude get people into serious trouble. Ignoring God never makes our lives smoother. The Israelites discovered that when each followed a selfish path and confusion ruled their nation.

Are you singing "I Did It My Way" or "I Did It His Way"? Which will be more successful? Determine to choose the way of the Father today.

Day 125

Judges 19:1–20:23; Luke 22:7–30; Psalm 77:1–11

[Jesus said,] "But you will not be like that. Let the greatest among you be as the least. Let the leader be as the one who cares for others."

LUKE 22:26

Not everyone is called to be a leader, but if you feel God's call, you are right to step out from the crowd and make it known. Just know that leadership in God's kingdom is a position of service. Like Moses and King David and Paul the apostle, God will humble you before He uses you. But if you're willing and obedient, He may use you to change the world.

Day 126

Judges 20:24–21:25; Luke 22:31–54;
Psalm 77:12–20

---

*You are the God who performs miracles;
you display your power among the peoples.*

PSALM 77:14 NIV

God works wonders in our hearts and lives and in the lives of believers around us. From these, do we recognize His strength, or are we simply seeking a form of spiritual entertainment? God doesn't do wonders in our hearts so that we alone feel His joy. Today, share His power with those around you, especially those who do not know His strength.

Day 127

Ruth 1–2; Luke 22:55–23:25; Psalm 78:1–4

"May the Lord reward you for your work.
May full pay be given to you from the Lord."
Ruth 2:12

Perhaps you feel unappreciated for the things you do for others—the cooking, cleaning, a late night at the office. Someone does take notice of all you do. Your heavenly Father is watching even when it seems no one notices. He's proud of you and appreciates all you do. You show the love and life of God to those around you. Take heart—God is your exceedingly great reward.

Day 128

But the other man on a cross spoke sharp words to the one who made fun of Jesus. He said, "Are you not afraid of God? You are also guilty and will be punished. We are suffering and we should, because of the wrong we have done. But this Man has done nothing wrong."

LUKE 23:40–41

🌿

"Not guilty!" That criminal on the cross next to Jesus knew the verdict He should have received. Do we? Or like the second criminal, are we so busy excusing our sins that we never understand the sacrifice that made forgiveness ours?

"Guilty!" Our verdict was never enforced; Jesus' love took our punishment. What sacrifice of ours could be large, compared to His?

Day 129

1 Samuel 1:1–2:21; Luke 24:13–53; Psalm 78:9–16

---

*The Lord made it possible for [Hannah]
to have a child, and when the time came
she gave birth to a son. She gave him
the name Samuel, saying, "I have
asked the Lord for him."*

1 Samuel 1:20

God wants us to pray, just as Hannah did in the Old Testament, and ask for the big things—like having a baby—and the little, everyday things. The next time you receive God's answer to a prayer, follow Hannah's example and acknowledge the fact that good gifts are from the Father.

Day 130

1 Samuel 2:22–4:22; John 1:1–28; Psalm 78:17–24

In the beginning was the Word, and the Word was with God, and the Word was God.

JOHN 1:1 KJV

Want a picture of God's Word? Look at Jesus, the embodiment of everything the Father wanted to say to us. You can't do that if you don't read the Book that tells of Him. Maybe that's why God takes it personally when we decide not to read His Word. We're pushing aside His love. God's scriptures communicate with His children. How can we know Him without His Word?

1 Samuel 5–7; John 1:29–51; Psalm 78:25–33

---

*But when they got up early the next morning,
they saw that Dagon had fallen on his face to
the ground in front of the special box of the
Lord. And Dagon's head and both his hands
were cut off and lying in the doorway.
Only the body of Dagon was left.*

1 Samuel 5:4

We may want to chuckle when we envision the idol Dagon flat on its face before the ark of the covenant. Daily the Philistine priests carefully placed him upright. But what of our own would-be idols? Each day will we prop up anything that seeks to take God's place in our lives, or will we allow it to fall flat before our Lord?

Day 132

1 Samuel 8:1–9:26; John 2; Psalm 78:34–41

When God began killing them,
they finally sought him.
They repented and
took God seriously.

PSALM 78:34 NLT

Does God have to allow disaster to happen before we recognize His power? Must our world be chaotic and dangerous before we seek our Savior? How much better to turn to Him before problems arise! Our Rock and Redeemer waits for us to turn in His direction. Don't make Him wait any longer!

Day 133

1 Samuel 9:27–11:15; John 3:1–22; Psalm 78:42–55

[Jesus said,] "For God so loved the world that He gave His only Son. Whoever puts his trust in God's Son will not be lost but will have life that lasts forever."

JOHN 3:16

Life on earth is fleeting. One day we're playing with our favorite dolls, and then we're adults dealing with grown-up issues. In a moment, we notice gray hair and wrinkles tickling the borders of our youthful faces. Life happens, and that's why God created a way for us to live on, free from time and age. Through His Son, He bought eternal life for you. What greater gift could there be?

Day 134

The Father loveth the Son,
and hath given all things into his hand.

JOHN 3:35 KJV

Young Christians often have a hard time connecting God the Father and Jesus. They trust the Son who saved them, but the Father may seem difficult to grasp.

Not to worry. There is no disconnect between Jesus and the Father. If you know the Savior, you know the One who sent Him. In loving Jesus, you've experienced the tender care of the Father who placed you in His hands. You love them both.

Day 135

1 Samuel 14; John 4:11–38; Psalm 78:67–72

He chose David, His servant and took him from the flocks of sheep. He brought him from caring for the sheep and their lambs to being the shepherd of Jacob His people, and Israel who belongs to Him.

PSALM 78:70–71

David certainly wasn't an impressive leader when the prophet Samuel anointed him king. He was just a lowly shepherd doing a messy, thankless job. But the lowly herder cared well for Israel.

Today too, God rarely chooses important people to do His will. He'd rather have faithful ones. Don't command that corner office or own a big house? Don't worry. God uses us "small" folks and rewards us in eternity.

Day 136

1 Samuel 15–16; John 4:39–54; Psalm 79:1–7

"For the Lord does not look at the things man looks at. A man looks at the outside of a person, but the Lord looks at the heart."

<small>1 Samuel 16:7</small>

When God looks at you, He sees a beautiful woman, a temple worthy of His Spirit. He sees your virtuous life and your godly attitudes. He sees a person whose heart has been washed clean and fully submitted to His will and purpose. He sees a beauty that is often missed by others. He sees an inner beauty. God sees you as you really are.

Day 137

1 Samuel 17; John 5:1-24; Psalm 79:8-13

Then David said to the Philistine, "You come to me with a sword and spears. But I come to you in the name of the Lord of All, the God of the armies of Israel, Whom you have stood against."

1 SAMUEL 17:45

We've heard the defiant words of unbelievers who attack and deny God. Do they shake our faith? Not if we recognize the incredible power of the Lord we serve. Like David, in faith we can face any doubter and declare His unchanging power.

Unbelievers come into our lives. What do they offer that is better than our Lord? Their names are nothing in comparison to the Savior's.

Day 138

1 Samuel 18–19; John 5:25–47; Psalm 80:1–7

---

*"You search the Scriptures because
you think they give you eternal life.
But the Scriptures point to me!"*

JOHN 5:39 NLT

Ever wondered how people like the Pharisees could quote scripture, yet be totally off base spiritually? Well, they didn't know the author of the Book. Reading the scriptures is good, but knowing the Master is even more important—simply memorizing His Word doesn't offer salvation. Without faith, God's Word is like speech to a deaf man. Today, take the time to read *and* hear His Word.

Day 139

1 Samuel 20–21; John 6:1–21; Psalm 80:8–19

"But if my father wants to hurt you, may the Lord do the same to Jonathan and even more, if I do not let you know and send you away, so you may be safe. May the Lord be with you as He has been with my father."

1 SAMUEL 20:13

When Jonathan supported David, he knew it meant he'd never sit on Israel's throne. He'd taken a dangerous step, but he loved and trusted his friend.

Do you have a Christian friend you trust this way? If so, you have a blessed relationship. Give thanks to God for providing you with such a worthwhile relationship.

Day 140

1 Samuel 22–23; John 6:22–42; Psalm 81:1–10

Sing aloud unto God our strength:
make a joyful noise unto the God of Jacob.

PSALM 81:1 KJV

Imagine you're in a room filled with noisy, fussy, crying children. The combination of their voices raised in miserable chorus is overwhelming. Now imagine that same group of children, singing praise to God in unison. They're making a joyful noise— and what a pleasant sound it is! Today, as you face life's many challenges, focus on being a praise giver, not a fussy child.

Day 141

1 Samuel 24:1–25:31; John 6:43–71;
Psalm 81:11–16

*"If only My people would listen to Me! . . .
I would hurry to crush those who fight
against them. I would turn My hand
against those who hate them."*

PSALM 81:13–14

Having one of those days? Does every enemy seem
to attack at once? Take heart, knowing God defends
those who hear His voice and walk in His ways.

Enemies who attack a faithful Christian have
their hands full. They aren't just fighting a frail
human, because God stands behind all those who
trust in Him. When He turns a hand against our
adversaries, they will not prevail.

Day 142

1 Samuel 25:32–27:12; John 7:1–24; Psalm 82

The brothers of Jesus said to Him,
"Leave here and go to the country of Judea.
Let Your followers there see the things You do."

JOHN 7:3

Sometimes well-meaning family members give just plain bad advice, as Jesus' brothers did when they advised Him to go openly to Jerusalem, though His life was endangered.

Bad advice doesn't mean these people don't love us; it means humans have limited knowledge and wisdom. Instead we need to rely on our source of unfailing wisdom: God's counsel never steers us wrong.

Day 143

1 Samuel 28–29; John 7:25–8:11; Psalm 83

[Jesus said,] "Let anyone who is thirsty come to me and drink. Whoever believes in me, as Scripture has said, rivers of living water will flow from within them."

JOHN 7:37–38 NIV

Ever been so thirsty that nothing could satisfy? You try everything within reach. You even try substitutes, but they're just that: a substitution for the real thing. Sometimes we have that deep-down soul-type thirst, seeking something in our life that will completely quench our parched soul. Jesus said that only He can satisfy that kind of thirst. He's there, no waiting. He can fill your life to overflowing.

Day 144

1 Samuel 30–31; John 8:12–47; Psalm 84:1–4

---

*[Jesus said,] And ye shall know the truth,
and the truth shall make you free.*

JOHN 8:32 KJV

Jesus is pure truth. If God lives in your heart, the blessing of truth is always available to you, helping you discern what is right for your life. Jesus never promised your pathway would be easy, but He has promised to never leave you. Truth is always with you. And you can call upon Him in every circumstance to light your way.

Day 145

2 Samuel 1–2; John 8:48–9:12; Psalm 84:5–12

For the Lord God is a sun and a safe-covering.
The Lord gives favor and honor. He holds back
nothing good from those who walk
in the way that is right.

PSALM 84:11

Lord, You position Yourself between us and sin. Oh, to be blameless. Oh, to always make the right choices. It's only through You that I can be blameless and forgiven. Lord, I recognize Your presence and ask Your forgiveness for all the times that I, like an errant child, didn't stay where I should.

Day 146

2 Samuel 3–4; John 9:13–34; Psalm 85:1–7

Ish-bosheth said to Abner, "Why have you gone in to the woman who acted as my father's wife?"

2 SAMUEL 3:7

Foolish words can change our lives forever, as Ish-bosheth discovered. These harsh words to his innocent uncle, who commanded Ish-bosheth's army, caused a split between them. Abner changed sides and supported David as king.

Do you make sure your information is correct before confronting someone? Or do you speak kindly because you're not certain? Let's speak softly and wisely and turn around a troubled relationship.

Day 147

2 Samuel 5:1–7:17; John 9:35–10:10;
Psalm 85:8–13

---

*[Jesus said,] "I have come that they may
have life, and have it to the full."*

JOHN 10:10 NIV

A baby spends nine months in her mother's womb becoming the person God has created her to be. In comparison to her life lived outside the womb, this preparation time is amazingly short. In the same way, our lives here on earth are relatively brief and intended as a time to grow and prepare for eternity with God. You are being groomed for eternal life with your Creator!

Day 148

2 Samuel 7:18–10:19; John 10:11–30;
Psalm 86:1–10

[Jesus said,] "My sheep hear My voice and I know them. They follow Me. I give them life that lasts forever. They will never be punished. No one is able to take them out of My hand."

<small>JOHN 10:27–28</small>

In eternity, we will have no need of protection. But here on earth, there are many dangers. God has not left your eternal life to chance. He purchased it for you with the sacrifice of His own Son, and He watches over you so that nothing and no one can keep you from reaching your destination. The life God has given you is sealed by His promise.

Day 149

2 Samuel 11:1–12:25; John 10:31–11:16;
Psalm 86:11–17

---

*But you, O Lord, are a God of compassion
and mercy, slow to get angry and filled
with unfailing love and faithfulness.*

PSALM 86:15 NLT

God never asks you to do anything for someone else
that He has not already done for you. You are able to
show compassion for others because He has shown
compassion for you. When you were sick with sin,
He forgave you. When your life was in shambles,
He held you close and comforted you. You give
from what you have already received.

Day 150

2 Samuel 12:26–13:39; John 11:17–54; Psalm 87

"Lord," Martha said to Jesus, "if you had been here, my brother would not have died."

JOHN 11:21 NIV

Martha and Mary knew Jesus could have healed their brother, Lazarus. But He wasn't there at the right moment. Do we know how they felt? We've all had moments when God felt distant. *Where did He go?* we may wonder. As with these sisters, He may be preparing something more wonderful—after all, Lazarus was resurrected!

Day 151

2 Samuel 14:1–15:12; John 11:55–12:19;
Psalm 88:1–9

---

*O Lord, the God Who saves me, I have cried
out before You day and night. Let my
prayer come to You. Listen to my cry.*

PSALM 88:1–2

"Listen, Lord!" the psalmist cried out to God. Though
the psalmist's life was incredibly challenging, God
didn't seem to hear. Did that mean the psalmist
stopped praying? No.

Like this psalmist, we need to remain persistent
in prayer. The God who saved us *will* answer—even
if it's not quite in the way we expected.

Day 152

2 Samuel 15:13–16:23; John 12:20–43;
Psalm 88:10–18

---

*[Jesus said,] "If anyone wants to serve Me,
he must follow Me. . . . If anyone serves
Me, My Father will honor him."*

JOHN 12:26

Serving God has no limits. No calling is too big or too small. Perhaps you're raising the next generation— your own children—to serve God. Maybe you speak to hundreds of thousands through books or on public platforms. Let your faith soar and remove anything that limits you. As you follow God, He will make the impossible possible. When you think you can, you can.

2 Samuel 17:1–18:18; John 12:44–13:20;
Psalm 89:1–6

---

*Now Ahithophel urged Absalom,
"Let me choose 12,000 men to
start out after David tonight."*

2 SAMUEL 17:1 NLT

Ahithophel offered Absalom shrewd battle advice,
but King David's son foolishly ignored it. Though
Ahithophel had been David's wisest adviser, God
supported His anointed king and ensured that
rebellious Absalom wouldn't heed his counselor.

Who gives wiser advice than God? Even astute
Ahithophel could not outdo His counsel. Nor will
our best advisers know more than the Lord of the
universe who sways all things to His will.

Day 154

2 Samuel 18:19–19:39; John 13:21–38;
Psalm 89:7–13

*"I give you a new Law. You are to love each
other. You must love each other as
I have loved you."*

JOHN 13:34

How do we know how to love? We learn from
Jesus. The Master had been with His disciples for
three years when He spoke these words, and they
had seen His love in action. We see it too in God's
Word and in the lives of faithful believers. We can
take what we know and follow Jesus, living out the
words He spoke and the good examples we have
seen.

Day 155

2 Samuel 19:40–21:22; John 14:1–17;
Psalm 89:14–18

Jesus said, "I am the Way and the Truth and the Life. No one can go to the Father except by Me."

<small>JOHN 14:6</small>

Plenty of people doubt Jesus. But those who have accepted Him as their Savior need not live in uncertainty. His Spirit speaks to ours if we will only listen. He tells us God has shown us the way; we need not seek another path or truth. No other road leads to God. For a vibrant Christian life, we simply need to continue down the highway we're traveling with Jesus.

Day 156

2 Samuel 22:1–23:7; John 14:18–15:27;
Psalm 89:19–29

*These things have I spoken unto you,
that my joy might remain in you,
and that your joy might be full.*

John 15:11 KJV

When you've been badly hurt, it's hard to let go
of the pain, isn't it? Sometimes it can crowd out
everything—your peace of mind, your enthusiasm,
your joy. If you're struggling with the effects of
a betrayal today, don't allow it to consume you.
Release it to God. Ask Him to replace the pain with
His joy—a joy that will remain in you, never to be
stolen again.

Day 157

2 Samuel 23:8–24:25; John 16:1–22;
Psalm 89:30–37

"When a woman gives birth to a child, she has sorrow because her time has come. After the child is born, she forgets her pain. She is full of joy because a child has been born into the world."

JOHN 16:21

If you've ever delivered a child, you know the pain associated with childbirth. But that's not what you remember after the fact. No, as you hold that little one in your arms, only one thing remains. . .the supernatural joy you experience as you gaze into your newborn's eyes. The same is true with the seasons we walk through. Sorrows will end, and joy will return once again!

Day 158

1 Kings 1; John 16:23–17:5; Psalm 89:38–52

"Until now you have not asked for anything in my name. Ask and you will receive, and your joy will be complete."

JOHN 16:24 NIV

Have you ever faced a truly impossible situation? One so extreme that, unless God moved, everything else would surely crumble? God is a God of the impossible. And He wants us to ask, even when we're facing insurmountable obstacles. In fact, He wants us to know that only He can perform miracles. Our job? We're called to trust Him. Then, when those impossible situations turn around, our joy will overflow!

Day 159

1 Kings 2; John 17:6–26; Psalm 90:1–12

---

*"I'm not asking you to take them out
of the world, but to keep them
safe from the evil one."*

JOHN 17:15 NLT

On tough days, Christians dream of escaping this sin-filled world. Though Jesus understood our trials, He didn't set up a Rapture for every trouble. Instead, He asked God to keep us from evil.

We can take this as God's word on the subject: we have more to do here, as long as He keeps us earthbound. So keep looking up—not for the Rapture, but for help from Jesus.

Day 160

1 Kings 3–4; John 18:1–27; Psalm 90:13–17

Let the favor of the Lord our God be upon us.
And make the work of our hands stand strong.
PSALM 90:17

Want your work to be effective? Don't make sure the boss knows every good thing you do. Seek God's favor, and He will see to it that your work really gets the job done, whether you're caring for a child, arguing a legal case, or waiting on a customer. Our Lord makes His people productive for Him as they serve others in His name.

Day 161

1 Kings 5–6; John 18:28–19:5; Psalm 91:1–10

He will cover you with His wings. And under His wings you will be safe. He is faithful like a safe-covering and a strong wall.

PSALM 91:4

Where are we safer than under God's wings? What trouble or doubt can harm us when He shields and protects us?

The Bible gives us three pictures of God's protection: the wings of a mother bird, a safe-covering (or shield), and a strong wall. How many ways can He tell us He guards us? When will we believe that nothing assails us that is greater than our Lord?

Day 162

1 Kings 7; John 19:6–24; Psalm 91:11–16

Pilate answered, "You take him and crucify him. As for me, I find no basis for a charge against him."

JOHN 19:6 NIV

No question about it: Pilate knew Jesus was innocent. Yet under pressure from the Jewish leaders, he handed Him over to injustice.

We may feel pressured to do wrong—in our families, at our jobs, or in the community. Do we avoid Pilate's mistake and stand firm? May we always seek God's defense instead of falling into evil.

Day 163

1 Kings 8:1–53; John 19:25–42; Psalm 92:1–9

"Now the Lord has kept His promise which He made. For I have taken my father David's place and sit on the throne of Israel, as the Lord promised. And I have built the house for the name of the Lord, the God of Israel."

1 KINGS 8:20

What an undertaking building that temple was! Today on earth, building a temple is just as difficult an undertaking because we are the temple. The struggle to maintain, uplift, and nurture self—let alone a family—to follow the Lord's teaching is what every modern-day Solomon strives for. Lord, help us remember God's promise of redemption. Help us to build our temples on the Rock.

Day 164

1 Kings 8:54–10:13; John 20:1–18; Psalm 92:10–15

Let your heart therefore be perfect with the
Lord our God, to walk in his statutes, and to
keep his commandments, as at this day.

1 Kings 8:61 kjv

Many women have issues with commitment. Their fear of failure causes them to drift in and out of relationships, jobs, and obligations without ever really settling anywhere. Committing your life first to God will help you commit later to others. Give Him your love, your life, your heart, and ask Him to help you walk out your commitment one day at a time. Everything else will follow.

Day 165

1 Kings 10:14–11:43; John 20:19–31; Psalm 93

Thy throne is established of old:
thou art from everlasting.

PSALM 93:2 KJV

There was never a moment when God did not exist. No scrap of time came into being without Him, and nothing escapes His powerful reign. That's good news for His children. For whatever we face, we know our Father is in control. No earthly disaster lies beyond His plan. No wickedness of Satan can take Him by surprise. Ours is the eternal Lord, who has loved us from the start.

Day 166

1 Kings 12:1–13:10; John 21; Psalm 94:1–11

"This is what the Lord says. 'You must not go up and fight against your brothers the sons of Israel. Every man return to his house. For I have let this thing happen.'"

1 Kings 12:24

What a shock to King Rehoboam when Israel made Jeroboam king. Wasn't Solomon's son entitled to the throne? Then God said it happened at His command.

We all have to be careful of our "entitlements." When, like Rehoboam, we treat people badly, we may lose our "rights." Our entitlement, if we have one, is to love others as God has loved us. Then we can never go wrong.

Day 167

But the LORD has become my fortress,
and my God the rock in whom I take refuge.

PSALM 94:22 NIV

Are you under attack by friends, family, or coworkers? If it comes because of your obedience to the Lord, stand firm in the face of their comments. He will defend you. If you face harsh words or nasty attitudes, remain kind, and He will assist you. Should your boss do you wrong, don't worry. Those who are against a Christian are also against Him, and God will make things right.

Day 168

1 Kings 15:1–16:20; Acts 1:12–26; Psalm 95

Let us come before Him giving thanks.
Let us make a sound of joy to Him with songs.
PSALM 95:2

Sometimes we forget that the Lord loves us to praise joyfully. We get caught up in tradition or maybe we just feel uncomfortable worshipping with abandon. The Lord loves a happy heart—and He truly enjoys it when we make a joyful noise, lifting up our praises (our psalms) for all to hear. So break out of the box today! Be set free. . .to worship!

Day 169

Others mocking said,
These men are full of new wine.
ACTS 2:13 KJV

No matter what wonderful thing God does, there will always be doubters. Tongues of fire resting on believers didn't change the hardened hearts of some who saw the Pentecost miracle.

First-century believers contended with doubters, and so will we. Like Peter, we can share the message, and some will believe, but only God changes hearts. Let's draw them to the Savior and leave the rest to Him.

Day 170

1 Kings 18:20–19:21; Acts 2:22–41;
Psalm 96:9–13

*"But God raised Him up. He allowed Him
to be set free from the pain of death.
Death could not hold its power over Him."*

ACTS 2:24

Death could not grasp Jesus, the sinless One who died for the guilty. Though it clings to sinful beings, it had no claim on God's Son. Jesus is our only hope. Though sin deserves death, God's compassion made a way to free us from its agonies. When we give our poor, mortal lives to Jesus, we rise in Him, sharing His eternal life.

Day 171

1 Kings 20; Acts 2:42–3:26; Psalm 97:1–6

"But you must be sorry for your sins and turn from them. You must turn to God and have your sins taken away. Then many times your soul will receive new strength from the Lord."

ACTS 3:19

When we consider repentance, we tend to think it's hard. That's only because we're shortsighted. Giving up sin may not appeal to our hardened hearts because we're not looking at the blessing set behind repentance. Yet as we turn from sin, we feel the refreshing breath of God's Spirit bringing new life to our lives. Then, does anything seem difficult?

Day 172

1 Kings 21:1–22:28; Acts 4:1–22; Psalm 97:7–12

Let those who love the Lord hate what is
bad. For He keeps safe the souls of His
faithful ones. He takes them away
from the hand of the sinful.

PSALM 97:10

Why do we hate evil? Not only because it's bad. We also don't want to run counter to God's plans. While He's working to guard and deliver us, why would we willingly walk right into Satan's trap?

Today, allow God to protect you from the evil you don't even know is on your doorsteps by doing what He wants—the first time!

Day 173

1 Kings 22:29–2 Kings 1; Acts 4:23–5:11;
Psalm 98

---

*Let the rivers clap their hands,
let the mountains sing together for joy.*

PSALM 98:8 NIV

All of nature sings the praises of our mighty God. Look around you! Do you see the hills off in the distance, pointing up in majesty? Can you hear the water in the brooks, tumbling along in a chorus of praise? And what about the ocean waves? Oh, the joy in discovering the God of the universe through His marvelous creation!

Day 174

2 Kings 2–3; Acts 5:12–28; Psalm 99

The soldiers said, "We found the door of the prison locked and the soldiers watching the doors. When we opened the door, we found no one inside."

ACTS 5:23

The Jewish officials were stunned. They'd had the apostles arrested and securely jailed, but when they called for them in the morning, the men had disappeared from the prison! Instead they were preaching in the temple courts.

Sometimes God does do amazing things in our lives. Are we stunned like the officials, or do we daily live in expectation of the wonderful things He accomplishes?

Day 175

2 Kings 4; Acts 5:29–6:15; Psalm 100

Make a joyful noise unto the LORD,
all ye lands.

PSALM 100:1 KJV

How do we praise God for His many blessings? If we follow the pattern of Old Testament saints, then we lift our voices in thanksgiving! We let others know. With a resounding voice, we echo our praises, giving thanks for all He has done and all He continues to do. So praise Him today! Make a joyful noise!

Day 176

*He made a big supper for them. When they
had eaten and drunk, he sent them away.
And they went to their owner. The Syrians
sent no more small groups of soldiers
into the land of Israel.*

2 KINGS 6:23

After God blinded them, Elisha captured these
Syrian warriors. He brought the soldiers to Israel's
king, who wanted to kill them. But the prophet
ordered them fed and sent home. Elisha's gentle
response brought peace between the nations.

Often a peaceful response gains more than
confrontation. Be ready to offer peace to your enemies today and every day.

2 Kings 6:24–8:15; Acts 7:17–36; Psalm 102:1–7

---

*I lie awake, lonely as
a solitary bird on the roof.*

PSALM 102:7 NLT

How perfectly the psalmist describes the loneliness of waking in the middle of the night. When the lights are out, we easily worry about our troubles. While those around us sleep, we experience wakefulness.

Be reminded that God does not sleep. No matter the hour, He hears our prayers. After we've shared our troubles, His renewing joy will come in the morning.

Day 178

2 Kings 8:16–9:37; Acts 7:37–53; Psalm 102:8–17

But You and Your name, O Lord, will always be forever and to all people for all time.

PSALM 102:12

When sin seems to rule the world, it's easy for us to feel tempted to believe that God's name will be forgotten on this earth. But that is only a ploy by Satan to stop us in our tracks.

God's name will always be lifted up by believers. Though others may deny Him, the faithful will always lift up His glory. How will you lift Him up today?

Day 179

2 Kings 10–11; Acts 7:54–8:8; Psalm 102:18–28

There was great joy in that city.
ACTS 8:8 KJV

Can you imagine the church of Jesus Christ—alive and vibrant in *every* city around the world? Alive in Moscow. Alive in Paris. Alive in Havana. Alive. . . in your hometown. Oh, the celebration that would ensue if cities around the world were eternally changed. Today, choose a particular city, and commit to pray for that place. . .that all might come to know Him!

Day 180

2 Kings 12–13; Acts 8:9–40; Psalm 103:1–9

*[The Lord] fills my years with good things and
I am made young again like the eagle.*

PSALM 103:5

God draws you close to Him because of the enormous wealth of love He has for you. The fresh scent that remains after a spring rain is an open invitation to rest in His mercy and grace. The flutter of a hummingbird's wings or the gentle sigh from a toddler's crib sends a special message that expresses His gentle desire to satisfy your heart with everything good.

Day 181

2 Kings 14–15; Acts 9:1–16; Psalm 103:10–14

Saul was still talking much about how he would like to kill the followers of the Lord.

ACTS 9:1

If anyone had a right to feel guilty, it was the apostle Paul. Before his conversion, he had a hand in killing God's people. But Paul never sat around mulling over past sins. He took God's forgiveness at face value and went to work for Him.

Is there a wrong you can't right? Maybe you need to follow Paul's example. Bemoaning past mistakes helps no one, but serving God will.

Day 182

2 Kings 16–17; Acts 9:17–31; Psalm 103:15–22

The loving-kindness of the Lord is forever and forever on those who fear Him. And what is right with God is given forever to their children's children.

PSALM 103:17

God loves you! It's not complicated or conditional—it's just a fact! Our human understanding can't comprehend the reason why, only that it's true. Instead of wrapping yourself in questions, wrap yourself in His love. Luxuriate in it just as you would a magnificent fur coat. God has spared no expense. He has given you the very best He has to offer.

Day 183

2 Kings 18:1–19:7; Acts 9:32–10:16;
Psalm 104:1–9

That ye may live, and not die.

2 KINGS 18:32 KJV

In life, there is really just one choice that matters. That is the choice of where you will spend eternity. God has given you a free will, and He expects you to use it. You must choose Him—consciously, intentionally choose Him—or you will be making a choice by default, a choice against Him. Your free will is His gift to you—use it!

Day 184

2 Kings 19:8–20:21; Acts 10:17–33;
Psalm 104:10–23

*He sends rivers into the valleys. They flow
between the mountains. They give water
to all the animals of the field.*

PSALM 104:10–11

God provides for animals by watering the valleys
and mountains where they live. Will He do less
for us? While we may not live beside a flowing
river, we also need His provision. Our same Lord
who sends the rain to water crops knows all about
our food bill. Just as He provided grass for ancient
Israel's cattle, He'll put bread, meat, and veggies
on our table.

Day 185

2 Kings 21:1–22:20; Acts 10:34–11:18;
Psalm 104:24–30

"I will not make the feet of Israel travel any more from the land I gave to their fathers. But they must obey all that I have told them, and all the Law that My servant Moses told to them."

God blesses any nation that follows Him, much the way He blessed Israel. But just as His ancient people slid away from real faith, modern nations easily lose their focus on Him and fall into depravity.

God's blessing doesn't rely on a nation's power or authority. It *does* depend on the obedience of those who trust in Him. How can we be more faithful today?

Day 186

2 Kings 23; Acts 11:19–12:17; Psalm 104:31–35

I will sing unto the LORD as long as I live: I will sing praise to my God while I have my being.

PSALM 104:33 KJV

Knowing Jesus isn't a passing phase, something we do before moving on to another activity. Pursuing God's will is a lifetime commitment that takes up every moment of our lives, if we allow it. As we draw our last breaths, if we've followed Him faithfully, we can give more fervent praise than we offered the first day we met our Lord. Do you want to join His eternal praise chorus?

Day 187

2 Kings 24–25; Acts 12:18–13:13; Psalm 105:1–7

Look to the LORD and his strength;
seek his face always.

PSALM 105:4 NIV

Have you ever tried to find someone in a crowd? You may be standing mere feet from each other, but the difficulty comes in seeing through the sea of bodies and voices. Like a crowd, our lives have lots of distractions vying for our attention. Take time today to push through all this and seek His face. Then keep your eyes on Him, no matter how large the crowd.

Day 188

1 Chronicles 1–2; Acts 13:14–43; Psalm 105:8–15

---

*"Men and brothers, listen to this.
You may be forgiven of your sins by this
One I am telling you about."*

ACTS 13:38

Forgiveness through Jesus is what Paul proclaimed to His people. God's grace appealed to many who heard him that day. But why didn't this whole synagogue come to Jesus? What could be simpler than simple acceptance of a Gospel message?

People have a strong desire to come to God on their own terms. Their pride keeps them from faith. Will it keep you from Him?

Day 189

1 Chronicles 3:1–5:10; Acts 13:44–14:10;
Psalm 105:16–28

---

*The disciples were filled with joy,
and with the Holy Ghost.*

ACTS 13:52 KJV

Want to know the secret of walking in the fullness of joy? Draw near to the Lord. Allow His Spirit to fill you daily. Let Him whisper sweet nothings in your ear and woo you with His love. The Spirit of God is your Comforter, your friend. He fills you to overflowing. Watch the joy flow!

Day 190

1 Chronicles 5:11–6:81; Acts 14:11–28;
Psalm 105:29–36

"He gave you rain from heaven and much food. He made you happy."

ACTS 14:17

When we think about provision, we usually think in terms of money. Getting the bills paid. Having food in the pantry. Making sure our needs are met. But what about our emotional needs? Does the Lord make provision in that area as well? Of course! According to this scripture, He fills our hearts with joy. What an awesome God we serve!

1 Chronicles 7:1–9:9; Acts 15:1–18;
Psalm 105:37–45

And he brought forth his people with joy,
and his chosen with gladness.

Psalm 105:43 kjv

Have you ever been delivered out of a terrible situation? Lifted out of it, unharmed? Were you stunned when it happened? Had you given up? God is in the deliverance business! And when He lifts us out of impossible situations, we are over-whelmed with joy. . .and we're surprised! Why do we doubt His goodness? The next time you're in a tough spot, expect to be "brought forth with joy."

Day 192

1 Chronicles 9:10–11:9; Acts 15:19–41;
Psalm 106:1–12

---

*Then they believed his promises
and sang his praise.*

PSALM 106:12 NIV

For almost every endeavor in life there are rules that should be followed. Too often, we want proof that there will be a reward before we make a true effort. Lord, Your promise is unfailing if we're only willing to believe and wait.

Day 193

1 Chronicles 11:10–12:40; Acts 16:1–15;
Psalm 106:13–27

They forgot the God Who saved them,
Who had done great things in Egypt.

PSALM 106:21

How could the Israelites who crossed the Red Sea forget the Lord who parted that water? Wouldn't that single miracle have gotten their attention for a lifetime? Proudly, we imagine we'd never have forgotten that! But is it true? He has given us just as great a miracle in the work of salvation in our lives. Let us always remember the Savior who died so we will never forget His love.

Day 194

1 Chronicles 13–15; Acts 16:16–40;
Psalm 106:28–33

*David told the heads of the Levites to choose
their brothers who sing and play music.
They were to play harps and timbrels
and make sounds of joy.*

1 CHRONICLES 15:16

It's tough to lift up your voice when you're feeling
down. Sometimes you just don't feel like praising.
However, coming together as a team—a group—
somehow boosts your strength! Once those instruments begin to play and the first few words of the
songs are sung, you're suddenly energized as never
before. So lift your voice with joy in the sanctuary!

Day 195

1 Chronicles 16–17; Acts 17:1–14;
Psalm 106:34–43

Honor and majesty surround him;
strength and joy fill his dwelling.

1 CHRONICLES 16:27 NLT

In Old Testament days, only the high priest could enter the Holy of Holies to spend intimate time with God. But when Jesus died on the cross, the veil in the temple was torn in two! We now have access to the Holy of Holies, and Jesus bids us enter. . .often! And oh, what joy when we enter in! Make that choice today.

Day 196

1 Chronicles 18–20; Acts 17:15–34;
Psalm 106:44–48

---

*For in him we live, and move,
and have our being.*

ACTS 17:28 KJV

✦

Every breath we breathe is a gift from our Creator.
We can do nothing apart from Him. In the same
sense, every joy, every sorrow. . .God goes through
each one with us. His heart is for us. We can experience joy in our everyday lives, even when things
aren't going our way. We simply have to remember
that He is in control. We live. . .in Him!

Day 197

1 Chronicles 21–22; Acts 18:1–23; Psalm 107:1–9

Give thanks to the Lord for He is good!
His loving-kindness lasts forever!
<small>PSALM 107:1</small>

When we lose a loved one or face some other terrible situation, we may wonder if the Lord we serve is really good. If He is, how could this happen to us?

God was good before our difficulties happened, and He's good today. Nothing changes His loving-kindness. He was good last month, yesterday, He is good today and will be good tomorrow and on into eternity. Give thanks, He *is* good!

Day 198

1 Chronicles 23–25; Acts 18:24–19:10;
Psalm 107:10–16

[Apollos] had been taught in the way of the Lord. And with a strong desire in his heart, he taught about Jesus. What he said was true, but he knew only about the baptism of John.

ACTS 18:25

Fervent faith is a good thing, but not if it speaks out of ignorance. Though Apollos had learned about the need for baptism, he had never encountered Jesus. So Priscilla and Aquila taught him the full story.

Do we speak fervently about truths we know little about? Maybe we need to study before we speak. Then when we share our testimony, faith and knowledge will be joined and effective.

1 Chronicles 26–27; Acts 19:11–22;
Psalm 107:17–32

*After this, Paul thought he would go through
the countries of Macedonia and Greece.
Then he would go to Jerusalem. He said,
"After I have been there, I must
go to the city of Rome also."*

ACTS 19:21

Paul had planned to visit Rome well before his travels brought him there. But never had he imagined that he'd go as a prisoner. When the apostle visited Jerusalem, his life changed drastically. But even in chains, God used Paul to spread His message.

Our lives too may take a sudden downward turn. Do we doubt God can still use us? Let's remember His servant Paul and take heart.

Day 200

1 Chronicles 28–29; Acts 19:23–41;
Psalm 107:33–38

---

*"I know, my God, that you test the heart
and are pleased with integrity."*

1 CHRONICLES 29:17 NIV

Everyone wants to be happy, right? We know that our obedience to the Lord results in a life of great joy. But our obedience does something else too. It brings pleasure to our heavenly Father. When we live uprightly, God is pleased. Today, instead of focusing on your own happiness, give some thought to putting a smile on *His* face.

Day 201

2 Chronicles 1–3; Acts 20:1–16;
Psalm 107:39–43

*"Now give me wisdom and much
understanding, that I may lead these people.
For who can rule this great nation of Yours?"*

2 Chronicles 1:10

When God asked Solomon what he wanted, the young king responded that he wanted wisdom. It was a good request from a humble man, so God gave him even more than he'd asked for. But Solomon didn't stay humble. Before long, he worshipped false gods.

Like Solomon, every Christian begins humbly, asking God's forgiveness. Will we stay the course of faith or end in error? Let's hold fast in faith today.

Day 202

"But I am not worried about this. I do not think of my life as worth much, but I do want to finish the work the Lord Jesus gave me to do. My work is to preach the Good News of God's loving-favor."

ACTS 20:24

The Christian life is a journey. We move from point A to point B—all the while growing in our faith. Instead of focusing on the ups and downs of the journey, we should be looking ahead, to the finish line. We want to be people who finish well. Today, set your sights on that unseen line that lies ahead. What joy will come when you cross it!

Day 203

2 Chronicles 6:12–7:10; Acts 21:1–14;
Psalm 109:1–20

"You have kept Your promises to Your servant
David my father. Yes, You have spoken with
Your mouth, and have done all You said
You would do, as it is today."

<small>2 Chronicles 6:15</small>

Oh Father, how often good intentions open our mouths. Promises of the mouth are easy; they take a second to make. Keeping those promises is hard. Fulfilling them takes more than a second. We often fail to keep promises. I'm so grateful You set the example. You humble us with Your fulfilled promises. You make us want to be better people.

Day 204

"But if you turn away and leave My Laws and My Word which I have given you, if you go and serve other gods and worship them, then I will take you from the land I have given you."

2 Chronicles 7:19–20

God gave Solomon a promise, and it wasn't a nice one. If the king turned from his faith, Israel would suffer. Solomon's faith did fail, and God fulfilled this promise during his son's reign.

What legacy will we leave our children? Will it be one of lifelong faith or a series of failures of belief that lead to disaster? Strong faith may be tested, but it never fails.

Day 205

2 Chronicles 9:29–12:16; Acts 21:33–22:16;
Psalm 110:1–3

---

*The Lord will send out Your strength
from Zion, saying, "Rule in front
of those who hate You."*

PSALM 110:2

Today, when we think of Jesus, we consider the suffering servant who died on the cross. But one day it will be different: the Father will send His Son as Lord to rule over all the earth.

We look forward to that day, but are we ready to bow the knee before our Lord? Are we serving Him wholeheartedly or expecting Him to serve us instead?

Day 206

2 Chronicles 13–15; Acts 22:17–23:11;
Psalm 110:4–7

*Be ye strong therefore, and let not your hands
be weak: for your work shall be rewarded.*

2 CHRONICLES 15:7 KJV

What is it that's threatening to make you give up?
Maybe it's exhaustion or discouragement. It might
be niggling questions like "Is this worth it? Is anyone going to notice?" Your determination will be
rewarded. God sees even if no one else does. He
understands the process and the difficulty. He will
be waiting at the finish line, and your efforts in this
life will be well worth it.

Day 207

The fear of the Lord is the beginning of wisdom. All who obey His Laws have good understanding. His praise lasts forever.

PSALM 111:10

God has answers to the questions you ask. You may find wisdom in a scripture that He prompts you to read, an insight in conversation with a friend. You need His wisdom every single day. God stands ready to assist. All you have to do is ask Him for help and then listen for the answer. Be encouraged—God has all the answers you need.

Day 208

2 Chronicles 18–19; Acts 24:22–25:12; Psalm 112

---

*"I saw the Lord sitting on His throne.
All the armies of heaven were standing
on His right and on His left."*

2 CHRONICLES 18:18

What do you think of when you hear the word *heaven*? What will it be like to walk on streets of gold, to see our loved ones who have gone before us? How thrilling, to know we will one day meet our Lord and Savior face-to-face. He has gone to prepare a place for us—and what a place it will be!

Day 209

*Then every man of Judah and Jerusalem
returned, with Jehoshaphat leading them.
They returned to Jerusalem with joy. For the
Lord had filled them with joy by saving
them from those who hated them.*

2 CHRONICLES 20:27

Enemy forces were just around the bend. Jehoshaphat, king of Judah, called his people together. After much prayer, he sent the worshippers (the Levites) to the front lines, singing joyful praises as they went. The battle was won! When you face your next battle, praise your way through it! Strength and joy will rise up within you! Prepare for victory!

[The Lord] turned the rock into a pool of water; yes, a spring of water flowed from solid rock.

PSALM 114:8 NLT

The psalmist, familiar with Israel's history, remembered that Moses hit a rock, and water flowed from it, quenching the thirst of God's people (Exodus 17:5–6).

Like Israel, we have dry times, when our world challenges us and our spirits feel parched. Will we seek the Lord's living water and drink our fill?

Day 211

2 Chronicles 24:1–25:16; Acts 27:1–20;
Psalm 115:1–10

---

*"Do not be afraid, Paul. You must stand in
front of Caesar. God has given you the
lives of all the men on this ship."*

ACTS 27:24

God didn't have to save the lives of the sailors who
brought Paul into this trouble by foolishly setting
sail in winter. The Lord could have plucked Paul
from the water and left the rest to drown. But by
His grace, each man came safely to shore.

How often have we seen God's grace work in
unbelievers' lives—perhaps through our prayers? Is
there someone you can pray for today?

Day 212

2 Chronicles 25:17–27:9; Acts 27:21–28:6;
Psalm 115:11–18

---

*As long as [King Uzziah] sought the L*ORD*,
God made him to prosper.*

2 CHRONICLES 26:5 KJV

Worldly success isn't always the most important focus of our lives, and God has many ways of prospering His people. But no matter whether we are kings like Uzziah or just ordinary folk, God can only truly prosper those who rely on Him.

Today, are you looking to the Lord? If so, whether it's fiscal, physical, or spiritual blessings, you can expect to be prosperous.

Day 213

2 Chronicles 28:1–29:19; Acts 28:7–31;
Psalm 116:1–5

---

*He kept on preaching about the holy nation
of God. He taught about the Lord Jesus
Christ without fear. No one stopped him.*

ACTS 28:31

Scripture doesn't tell us just how Paul's life ended,
but it does tell us how he continued his mission
in this last verse of the book of Acts. Carried to
Rome, following his appeal to Caesar for justice,
Paul fearlessly taught about Jesus.

No matter what changes in life, determine to
continue in your mission for God. No trouble can
separate you from Him if you follow faithfully.

Day 214

2 Chronicles 29:20–30:27; Romans 1:1–17;
Psalm 116:6–19

*You have been chosen to
belong to Jesus Christ.*

ROMANS 1:6

Legos are fascinating toys. They come in various sizes and shapes. Some Legos fit anywhere. Others have specific functions. Try to force them in the wrong place and you wind up with an awkward structure or one that tumbles. Lord, I want to be like that Lego that knows where it belongs. If I stumble down the wrong road, let me feel awkward so that I turn around before I fall.

Day 215

2 Chronicles 31–32; Romans 1:18–32; Psalm 117

O praise the LORD, all ye nations:
praise him, all ye people.
PSALM 117:1 KJV

Can you imagine the sound of millions of people, singing praises to the Lord in thousands of different languages at once? Every day, God hears people all over the world lift up their praises to Him in their native tongues. Today, as you lift your voice, think of the millions of others who join you. Praise Him! Oh, praise Him!

Day 216

2 Chronicles 33:1–34:7; Romans 2;
Psalm 118:1–18

---

*When [Manasseh] prayed to Him, God heard
his prayer and listened to him, and brought
him again to Jerusalem and to his nation.
Then Manasseh knew that the Lord was God.*

2 CHRONICLES 33:13

Have you ever felt too unworthy for God to hear
your prayers? Manasseh had every reason to feel
this way. This boy-king of Israel built altars to
heathen gods, worshipped stars in the sky, and
practiced witchcraft. But when this misguided ruler
turned from his sin and dropped to his knees in
prayer, God listened and answered. He'll do the
same for you when you seek Him.

Day 217

2 Chronicles 34:8–35:19; Romans 3:1–26;
Psalm 118:19–23

I will give you thanks, for you answered me;
you have become my salvation.

PSALM 118:21 NIV

A new believer didn't write this verse. The psalmist thanks God not just for loving him enough to tear him from the claws of original sin; instead, this mature man of faith recognizes that God saves him every day, whenever he is in trouble. God does this in your life too. What salvation has He worked in your life recently? What thanks do you need to offer Him now?

Day 218

2 Chronicles 35:20–36:23; Romans 3:27–4:25;
Psalm 118:24–29

---

*This is the day which the L*ORD *hath made;
we will rejoice and be glad in it.*

PSALM 118:24 KJV

Are you having a hard day? Facing mounting problems? Maybe the bill collectors are calling or the kids are sick. You're at the end of your rope. Pause for a moment and remember: "This is the day which the Lord has brought about. I *will* rejoice." It's His day, and He longs for you to spend time with Him. Rejoice! It's the right choice.

Day 219

Ezra 1–3; Romans 5; Psalm 119:1–8

Hope never makes us ashamed because the love of God has come into our hearts through the Holy Spirit Who was given to us.

ROMANS 5:5

Tired of being disappointed time and time again? Ready for things to change? Try hope. Hope never leads to disappointment. When you're hopeful, you are anticipating good things, not bad. And even if the "good things" you're waiting on don't happen right away, you're energized with joy until they do. So wave goodbye to disappointment. Choose hope. Choose joy.

Day 220

Ezra 4–5; Romans 6:1–7:6; Psalm 119:9–16

We were buried in baptism as Christ was buried in death. As Christ was raised from the dead by the great power of God, so we will have new life also.

ROMANS 6:4

Baptism is a picture of the old, sinful nature's death and the new faith-life God gives those who trust in Him. Belief in Jesus has a life-altering impact. One moment, a sinful person is dead, held in sin's grasp. The next, she becomes an entirely new person, alive in her Savior. Only Jesus offers this glorious freedom. Has He given it to you?

Day 221

Ezra 6:1–7:26; Romans 7:7–25; Psalm 119:17–32

---

*Whatsoever is commanded by the God
of heaven, let it be diligently done.*

EZRA 7:23 KJV

One of the many ways to worship God is to give—
until it hurts. Maybe He's calling you to spend
your time with society's rejects; maybe your heart
is telling you to sell your DVD collection and give
the money to further God's kingdom on earth.
Whatever it is that God wants from you, let it be
done in full and all to His glory.

Day 222

Ezra 7:27–9:4; Romans 8:1–27; Psalm 119:33–40

Now, because of this, those who belong to Christ will not suffer the punishment of sin.

ROMANS 8:1

No punishment! What a wonderful thought for sinners! Forgiven, we know the comfort of having heaven as our ultimate destination. But have we also read the second part of the verse? This is no blanket agreement that okays sin. The joy of our freedom must lead us to turn from all wrong. Our Lord gives the strength to grow in Him.

Day 223

Ezra 9:5–10:44; Romans 8:28–39;
Psalm 119:41–64

For I know that nothing can keep us from the love of God. Death cannot! Life cannot! . . . Any other power cannot! Hard things now or in the future cannot! . . . Any other living thing cannot keep us away from the love of God which is ours through Christ Jesus our Lord.

Romans 8:38–39

You don't have to be alone to feel lonely. Perhaps you feel no one understands you and no one cares. This time in your life probably won't last long. You will make connections and the loneliness will pass, but until it does, remember that God has promised to always be there for you—to listen, to comfort, to encourage. He's as close as your prayer.

Day 224

Nehemiah 1:1–3:16; Romans 9:1–18;
Psalm 119:65–72

*When I heard these things, I sat down and
wept. For some days I mourned and fasted
and prayed before the God of heaven.*

NEHEMIAH 1:4 NIV

Bad news. When it arrives, what's your reaction? To scream? Fall apart? Run away? Nehemiah's response to bad news was a model for us. First, he vented his sorrow. It's okay to cry and mourn. Christians suffer pain like everyone else; only we know the source of inner healing. Like Nehemiah, our next step is to turn to the only true source of help and comfort.

Day 225

Nehemiah 3:17–5:13; Romans 9:19–33;
Psalm 119:73–80

---

*May those who fear You see me and be glad,
for I have put my hope in Your Word.*

PSALM 119:74

Have you ever met someone you immediately knew was filled with joy? The kind of effervescent joy that bubbles up and overflows, covering everyone around her with warmth and love and acceptance? We love to be near people filled with Jesus joy. And even more, as Christians we want to be *like* them!

Day 226

Nehemiah 5:14–7:73; Romans 10:1–13;
Psalm 119:81–88

*"No one who puts his trust in Christ
will ever be put to shame."*

ROMANS 10:11

As you look back on your life, recall the times you placed hope and confidence in God. The outcome might not have been exactly as you imagined, but God is always faithful to bring you through. Whatever you're facing today, you can rest assured that His blessings will never stop. He will walk it out with you—every step of the way.

Day 227

Nehemiah 8:1–9:5; Romans 10:14–11:24;
Psalm 119:89–104

For ever, O LORD,
thy word is settled in heaven.
PSALM 119:89 KJV

God's Word never changes. The Father's commands do not alter, and neither does Jesus, the Word made flesh, or His promise of salvation. Those who trust in Him are secure as the Lord Himself, for He does not change, and none of His promises pass away unfulfilled. The eternal Lord and all He commands stand firm. To gain eternity, simply receive Christ as your Savior; then trust in Him.

Day 228

Nehemiah 9:6–10:27; Romans 11:25–12:8;
Psalm 119:105–120

*We all have different gifts that God has
given to us by His loving-favor.*

ROMANS 12:6

God has blessed every person—every single one—
with some gift or ability we can use to serve others
and bring glory to His name. Some abilities are
obvious—they shine brightly in front of everyone—
but others move below the radar: the ability to pray
effectively, love the unlovely, listen attentively. Ask
God to open your eyes to your special abilities. They
are God's blessings to you.

Day 229

Nehemiah 10:28–12:26; Romans 12:9–13:7;
Psalm 119:121–128

Rejoice in our confident hope. Be patient in trouble, and keep on praying.

ROMANS 12:12 NLT

The words *rejoice* and *hope* just seem to go together, don't they? There's something about choosing joy that fills our hearts with hope for better days ahead. If we have to wait awhile, so what? If we stay focused on the Lord, casting our cares on Him, that day of rejoicing will surely come!

Day 230

Nehemiah 12:27–13:31; Romans 13:8–14:12;
Psalm 119:129–136

Order my steps in thy word.
PSALM 119:133 KJV

Scripture tells us that God's Word is "a lamp to my feet and a light to my path" (Psalm 119:105), but that's just the beginning of the journey. Once we see the light the Bible offers, it's up to us to take the first step in the right direction. While we'll always have free will when it comes to decisions, God promises to prepare the pathway in His Word.

Day 231

Esther 1:1–2:18; Romans 14:13–15:13;
Psalm 119:137–152

---

*Our hope comes from God. May He fill you
with joy and peace because of your trust in
Him. May your hope grow stronger by
the power of the Holy Spirit.*

ROMANS 15:13

Isn't it fun to think about God pouring joy into
our lives? Imagine yourself with a water pitcher in
hand, pouring out, out, out. . .covering everything
in sight. The Lord wants us, through the power of
the Spirit, to overflow. To bubble over. To experience joy and hope. Today, as you spend time in
prayer, allow God to saturate you with His joyous
hope.

Day 232

Esther 2:19–5:14; Romans 15:14–21;
Psalm 119:153–168

*"Who knows if you have not become
queen for such a time as this?"*
ESTHER 4:14

Crowned queen after winning a beauty contest, Esther was only allowed audience with her king when summoned. When Esther learned of a plot to destroy her people, she faced a tough decision. She was the *only* one who could save them—at supreme risk. God had intentionally placed her in that position for such a time. What's your divinely ordained position?

Day 233

Esther 6–8; Romans 15:22–33;
Psalm 119:169–176

*I am made happy by Your Word,
like one who finds great riches.*

PSALM 119:162

Have you ever read scripture with the anticipation of finding something truly amazing? We're all guilty of becoming apathetic about God's Word. The truth is that the Bible offers something greater than riches—the power of heavenly wisdom and guidance. Learn the truths of God, hide them in your heart, and you'll be rich for eternity.

Day 234

Esther 9–10; Romans 16; Psalm 120–122

Everyone knows you have obeyed the teaching you received. I am happy with you because of this. But I want you to be wise about good things and pure about sinful things.

ROMANS 16:19

Ever been caught in a situation where people were talking about you behind your back? Maybe folks you loved and trusted? How did that make you feel? Well, how would you feel if you found out people were talking about you. . .because of your obedience? Wow! That's a different thing altogether. Let them talk! May our joyful obedience to the Lord win us a spot in many cheerful conversations!

Day 235

Job 1–3; 1 Corinthians 1:1–25; Psalm 123

In His wisdom, He did not allow man to come to know Him through the wisdom of this world. It pleased God to save men from the punishment of their sins through preaching the Good News. This preaching sounds foolish.

1 CORINTHIANS 1:21

To this world, God's wisdom doesn't look very wise. Anyone who denies Jesus is blind to the depth of insight God showed in sending His Son to die for us and then raising Him from the dead. But those who accept His sacrifice understand that God's ways are greater than ours. As His wisdom fills our once foolish lives, we gain a new perspective on His perception.

Day 236

Our help is in the name of the Lord,
who made heaven and earth.

Psalm 124:8 KJV

The name God told to Moses, "I AM WHO I AM," describes His unchanging nature. So here, when the Unchanging One promises to help us, that assurance never alters. What in heaven or on earth could be too powerful or too much trouble for its Maker? Nothing is greater than God, not even our biggest challenge. We need only call His name.

Day 237

Job 7–9; 1 Corinthians 3; Psalm 126–127

Do you not know that you are a house of God and that the Holy Spirit lives in you?

1 Corinthians 3:16

God lives within you, not in a distant place. When you act according to His Word, He acts. When you fail, people may begin to doubt Him. That's why Paul encourages you to live devotedly for your Lord. As one of His people, you're filled with His potent Spirit, who empowers you to live a holy life. Live in His strength always.

Day 238

Job 10–13; 1 Corinthians 4:1–13; Psalm 128–129

For you will eat the fruit of your hands.
You will be happy and it will be well with you.

PSALM 128:2

We're always waiting for the payoff, aren't we? When we've put a lot of effort into a project, we hope to see good results. The Word of God promises that we will eat the fruit of our labor—that we will eventually experience blessings and prosperity. So all of that hard work will be worth it. But remember, the joy is in the journey!

Day 239

Job 14–16; 1 Corinthians 4:14–5:13; Psalm 130

---

*Let Israel hope in the LORD: for with the
LORD there is mercy, and with him
is plenteous redemption.*

PSALM 130:7 KJV

Why hope in God, even in dire situations? Because every one of His people greatly needs His overflowing mercy. Our lives are frail, but He is not. Jesus brings the redemption we require. No matter what we face, Jesus walks with us. We need only trust faithfully that His salvation is on the way.

Day 240

Job 17–20; 1 Corinthians 6; Psalm 131

"Where then is my hope?"
JOB 17:15 NLT

On hectic days when fatigue takes its toll, hope disappears. When hurting people hurt people and we're in the line of fire, hope vanishes. When ideas fizzle, efforts fail, we throw the spaghetti against the wall and nothing sticks, hope seems lost. But we must remember it's only temporary. The mountaintop isn't gone just because it's obscured by fog; visibility will improve tomorrow. And hope will rise.

Day 241

Job 21–23; 1 Corinthians 7:1–16; Psalm 132

I will give her many good things.
I will give her poor people much bread.

PSALM 132:15

The Lord has promised to meet all of our needs, according to His riches in glory. His heart is for His people, especially the poor and downtrodden. Today, as you seek God about your own needs, ask Him how you can help meet the needs of the less fortunate in your community. What a joy it will be, to reach out to others. . .even if you're also in need.

Day 242

Job 24–27; 1 Corinthians 7:17–40; Psalm 133–134

I want you to be free from the cares of this world. The man who is not married can spend his time working for the Lord and pleasing Him.

1 CORINTHIANS 7:32

There is a season for everything on earth—including singleness. Whether you remain single throughout your life or choose to marry, singleness is a special time, a time when you are free to grow and learn and draw closer to God. Many singles miss these treasures because they are focused on the future. Rejoice in the now. See what God has in store for you today.

Day 243

Job 28–30; 1 Corinthians 8; Psalm 135

*I know that the LORD is great,
and that our Lord is above all gods.*

PSALM 135:5 KJV

Other "gods" contend with Jesus in the market-place of ideas, and devout Christians may encounter contention. But just as the psalmist recognized God's greatness, we can too as we look at the world around us. No other would-be deity shows forth its glory in creation. No other has provided His gracious salvation. If our Lord controls our lives, how can we look to any other gods?

Day 244

Job 31–33; 1 Corinthians 9:1–18; Psalm 136:1–9

Give thanks to the God of gods,
for His loving-kindness lasts forever.

PSALM 136:2

Having trouble being thankful? Read Psalm 136. You'll be reminded of the wonders of God's power and His enduring love. The God who protected Israel watches over you too. Even when there may be little in your life to rejoice about, you can always delight in Him. Give thanks to God. He has not forgotten you—His love endures forever.

Day 245

Job 34–36; 1 Corinthians 9:19–10:13;
Psalm 136:10–26

You have never been tempted to sin in any different way than other people. God is faithful. He will not allow you to be tempted more than you can take. But when you are tempted, He will make a way for you to keep from falling into sin.

1 CORINTHIANS 10:13

No matter how powerful it seems, you need not give in to temptation. God always provides you with an escape hatch. When temptation pulls at you, turn your eyes to Jesus. Replace that tempting object with Him, and you will not fall.

Day 246

Job 37–39; 1 Corinthians 10:14–11:1; Psalm 137

"Who provides food for the raven when its young cry out to God and wander about for lack of food?"

JOB 38:41 NIV

Does it fill your heart with joy to know that God provides for your needs? He makes provision. . .both in seasons of want and seasons of plenty. There's no need to strive. No need to worry. He's got it all under control. If He provides food for the ravens, then surely He knows how to give you everything you need when you need it. So praise Him!

Day 247

Job 40–42; 1 Corinthians 11:2–34; Psalm 138

"I had heard of You only by the hearing of the ear, but now my eye sees You."

Job 42:5

As children we sang, "Jesus loves me," and we believed because, well, we were told to. But as adults we reach a crossroads: either pull on the boots of faith and take ownership or simply polish them occasionally, maybe at Easter and Christmas, as they sit neglected and dusty in the closet. Have you taken ownership of your faith? Go ahead, sister, those boots were made for walkin'!

Day 248

Ecclesiastes 1:1–3:15; 1 Corinthians 12:1–26;
Psalm 139:1–6

*The Holy Spirit works in each person in one
way or another for the good of all.*

1 CORINTHIANS 12:7

Did you know that you are a gifted person? God gives each of His children spiritual gifts designed to help themselves and others—wisdom, knowledge, faith, healing, to name just a few. As you grow spiritually, you begin to unwrap those presents from God. Over time, you may be surprised and blessed at how many He's provided for you.

Feeling unimportant? Remind yourself that you're gifted by God!

Day 249

Ecclesiastes 3:16–6:12;
1 Corinthians 12:27–13:13; Psalm 139:7–18

Love does not give up. Love is kind. Love is not jealous. Love does not put itself up as being important. Love has no pride.

1 Corinthians 13:4

God's love is not short tempered or short lived. Unlike human love, it never gives up on you, even on those long, discouraging days when your job is a strain, family life becomes confused, and you hardly know where to turn. In such stressful times, your heavenly Father puts up with all of it, right beside you. He's not out there somewhere—He's close by your side.

Day 250

Ecclesiastes 7:1–9:12; 1 Corinthians 14:1–22;
Psalm 139:19–24

---

*Go and eat your bread in happiness.
Drink your wine with a happy
heart. For God has already been
pleased with your works.*

ECCLESIASTES 9:7

Ever feel like nothing you do is good enough?
Your boss is frustrated over something you've done
wrong. The kids are complaining. Your neighbors
are even upset at you. How wonderful to read
that God accepts our works, even when we feel
lacking. He encourages us to go on our way with
a merry heart, completely confident that we are
accepted by Him.

Day 251

Ecclesiastes 9:13–12:14;
1 Corinthians 14:23–15:11; Psalm 140:1–8

Honor God and obey His Laws.
This is all that every person must do.

ECCLESIASTES 12:13

❦

God knows how busy your life is. As you move from task to task, remember to hold on to the golden cord that connects you to Him. He's always there regardless, but the cord reminds you that He is. It keeps the conversation going between the two of you and His love, joy, and peace flowing to you throughout your day. God should be your first priority because it is through His wisdom and strength that you accomplish the others.

Day 252

Song of Solomon 1–4; 1 Corinthians 15:12–34;
Psalm 140:9–13

---

*Surely the righteous shall give thanks unto thy
name: the upright shall dwell in thy presence.*

PSALM 140:13 KJV

Have you ever gone camping in a tent? What if you
had a special place—a quiet, private place like that
tent—where you could dwell with God? A private
place of worship? Wouldn't you want to linger
inside that holy habitat, separating yourself from
the outside world? Pitch your tent today. . .and
spend some time inside with the King of kings.

Day 253

Song of Solomon 5–8; 1 Corinthians 15:35–58;
Psalm 141

---

*But God is the One Who gives us power
over sin through Jesus Christ our Lord.
We give thanks to Him for this.*

1 Corinthians 15:57

What a wonderful, giving God we serve. He stands with an extended hand, ready to give you the desires of your heart. Take a moment to offer thanks to Him for the greatest gifts and even the small things that you realize He engineered to bless you in an unexpected way. Share with Him just how much He means to you. He is worthy of your thanks.

Day 254

Isaiah 1–2; 1 Corinthians 16; Psalm 142

Be on guard. Stand firm in the faith.
Be courageous. Be strong.
1 CORINTHIANS 16:13 NLT

Being a Christian can take lots of courage. As the world around us becomes increasingly hostile to God, we feel the challenge. But we are not defenseless. Christians through the ages have faced these troubles and triumphed. The Lord who supported them gives us strength too. Let us stand fast for Jesus, calling on His Spirit to strengthen our lives. Then we will be strong indeed.

Day 255

Isaiah 3–5; 2 Corinthians 1:1–11; Psalm 143:1–6

*As we have suffered much for Christ and
have shared in His pain, we also
share His great comfort.*

2 CORINTHIANS 1:5

Paul knew the pain of persecution, but he also knew
the deep comfort God offered. When people gave
the apostle trouble, God drew His servant close to
His heart. When trials come your way, God will do
the same for you. If life is always going smoothly,
comfort is meaningless, but when you're in the midst
of trouble, He comes alongside with tender love that
overflows your trials.

Day 256

Isaiah 6–8; 2 Corinthians 1:12–2:4;
Psalm 143:7–12

---

*God is the One Who makes our faith and
your faith strong in Christ. He has set us apart
for Himself. He has put His mark on us
to show we belong to Him. His Spirit
is in our hearts to prove this.*

2 Corinthians 1:21–22

The last time you applied for a loan, were you preapproved? Good feeling, isn't it? You have been preapproved for God's kingdom. He's given you His Word and stamped you with His eternal pledge. You belong to Him. He is fully committed to helping you become all you were created to be. He will never turn His back on you.

Day 257

Isaiah 9–10; 2 Corinthians 2:5–17; Psalm 144

Now thanks be unto God, which always causeth us to triumph in Christ.

2 CORINTHIANS 2:14 KJV

God has created us to be victors, not victims. We are image bearers of Christ and born to triumph! So how do you see yourself today? Have you made up your mind to overcome in the areas where you've struggled? One way to assure your victory is to praise God for it. . .even before it happens. That's right! Praise your way through! Oh, the joy of triumphing in Christ!

Day 258

Isaiah 11–13; 2 Corinthians 3; Psalm 145

---

*As water from a well brings joy to the thirsty,
so people have joy when He saves them.*

ISAIAH 12:3

In biblical times, women drew water from wells. They would drop the bucket down, down, down, then lift it up again, filled to the brim. The Lord wants you to reach down into His well of salvation and, with great joy, draw up the bucket. Remember how He saved you? Remember His grace? Is your bucket filled to the brim? If so, then that's something to celebrate!

Day 259

Isaiah 14–16; 2 Corinthians 4; Psalm 146

Our human body is wearing out.
But our spirits are getting stronger every day.

2 CORINTHIANS 4:16

Your relationship with God is alive. It's living and breathing and requires nourishment to survive. Much like how tributaries pour into lakes and rivers, you give out of your spirit into all you do. When you give out, you can drain your reserves. God wants you full. Fill up as you renew your spirit and mind daily with His Word and in His presence. You're a life-giving river of living water. Fill up, pour out, and fill up again!

Day 260

Isaiah 17–19; 2 Corinthians 5; Psalm 147:1–11

For if a man belongs to Christ, he is a new person. The old life is gone. New life has begun.

2 CORINTHIANS 5:17

New life in Christ: what indescribable freedom to be separated from our sin! No longer bound by it but able to live in Him, we joyfully race into our new existence. But in time, our tendency to fall into sin tarnishes God's gift. Suddenly we don't feel so new. "Old" Christians need only turn again to Christ for forgiveness, and the Spirit's cleansing makes us new again.

Day 261

Isaiah 20–23; 2 Corinthians 6; Psalm 147:12–20

---

*"I will be a Father to you. You will be My sons
and daughters, says the All-powerful God."*
2 CORINTHIANS 6:18

Only unconfessed sin can separate you from the
Father. But God never desires such distance. He
wants to draw near, like a loving Father who holds
His child, provides for her, and helps her at every
turn. He heals your hurts, solves your problems,
and offers His love at every turn. All you need to do
is turn to Him in love.

Day 262

Isaiah 24:1–26:19; 2 Corinthians 7; Psalm 148

---

*Godly sorrow brings repentance that leads
to salvation and leaves no regret.*

2 CORINTHIANS 7:10 NIV

Godly sorrow accompanies the pain of our own sins. When we know that our actions have hurt us, others, and even the heart of God, we need to do something about it. We repent, and God offers His salvation. Has sin come between you and your Savior? Turn at once in sorrow and ask Him to make everything right in your heart and soul. You'll never be sorry you did.

Day 263

Isaiah 26:20–28:29; 2 Corinthians 8;
Psalm 149–150

---

*They gave not only what they could afford,
but far more. And they did it of
their own free will.*

2 CORINTHIANS 8:3 NLT

Have you ever felt like giving, just to bless someone? Just to bring joy to a friend's heart? Just to lift
a burden? There's something rather exciting about
giving in secret, isn't there? And when you reach
way down deep—giving out of your own need—it's
even more fun. Today, take inventory of the people
in your life. Who can you bless. . .in secret?

Day 264

Isaiah 29–30; 2 Corinthians 9; Proverbs 1:1–9

The man who plants only a few seeds will not have much grain to gather. The man who plants many seeds will have much grain to gather.

2 CORINTHIANS 9:6

What you give is what you get. That's true in life, and it's also true spiritually. Anyone who tries to hold her finances close will be letting go of spiritual blessings, while the person who shares generously gains in so many ways. It's hard to give up worldly treasures, but when you give in the name of Jesus, you will never run short.

Day 265

Isaiah 31–33; 2 Corinthians 10;
Proverbs 1:10–22

---

*We break down every thought and proud
thing that puts itself up against the wisdom
of God. We take hold of every thought
and make it obey Christ.*

2 Corinthians 10:5

God gave you a mind equipped with an amazing ability to think and reason. Your thoughts are the starting point of every decision you make. Your loving heavenly Father gave you guidelines in His Word to help you determine the direction your thoughts should take. He created you to fulfill your every dream. Think higher—His way of thinking produces peace, health, prosperity, wisdom, and so many blessings.

Day 266

Those whom the Lord has paid for and set free will return. . . . Joy that lasts forever will crown their heads. They will be glad and full of joy. Sorrow and sad voices will be gone.

ISAIAH 35:10

Have you ever pondered eternity? Forever and ever and ever . . . ? Our finite minds can't grasp the concept, and yet one thing we understand from scripture—we will enter eternity in a state of everlasting joy and gladness. No more tears! No sorrow! An eternal joy-fest awaits us! Now that's something to celebrate!

Day 267

Isaiah 37–38; 2 Corinthians 12:1–10;
Proverbs 1:27–33

---

*I receive joy when I am weak. I receive joy
when people talk against me and make it hard
for me and try to hurt me and make trouble
for me. I receive joy when all these things
come to me because of Christ. For when
I am weak, then I am strong.*

2 CORINTHIANS 12:10

Only God can make you strong in the weak places. In those spots of persecution and hardship, His power and grace shine through your fragile vessel as you live as a faithful Christian. When you feel broken and useless, trust in Him to fill your flaws, and His light will shine through the cracks of your pain and reach a hurting world.

Day 268

Isaiah 39–40; 2 Corinthians 12:11–13:14;
Proverbs 2:1–15

*For the LORD giveth wisdom: out of his mouth
cometh knowledge and understanding.*

PROVERBS 2:6 KJV

Have you ever had that feeling deep in your gut
that you should—or shouldn't—do something?
The Holy Spirit dwells within you, ready to give
you the wisdom you need to make good choices.
If you're listening, you will hear Him. He won't
shout or force you to hear what He has to say. The
more you trust His lead, the more you will grow
in wisdom.

Day 269

Isaiah 41–42; Galatians 1; Proverbs 2:16–22

"He will not lose hope or be crushed, until He has made things right on the earth. And the islands will wait with hope in His Law."

ISAIAH 42:4

Change—besides our unalterable Lord—is the only thing constant in this world. Yet the only person who likes change is a baby with a wet diaper. Isaiah prophesied that the Almighty will one day create positive change on earth. Like the tides that clean beach debris after a storm, positive change washes away the old and refreshes with the new. In this we hope.

Day 270

Isaiah 43:1–44:20; Galatians 2; Proverbs 3:1-12

"See, I will do a new thing. It will begin happening now. Will you not know about it? I will even make a road in the wilderness, and rivers in the desert."

ISAIAH 43:19

Some evenings bring a breathtaking orange sunset. The amazing thing about this is that the vibrant color comes from pollution. How can it be, Lord, that Your splendor overcomes such obstacles as the impurities in the air? How can it be, Lord, that You see past our imperfections and Your grace allows us to start anew? How can it be? It is the love of the Father.

Day 271

Isaiah 44:21–46:13; Galatians 3:1–18;
Proverbs 3:13–26

---

*No one is made right with God by doing
what the Law says. For, "The man right
with God will live by faith."*

GALATIANS 3:11

Though some might claim it, crossing all your t's and dotting your i's spiritually does not make you a great Christian. Rules and regulations aren't what the Christian life is about—faith is. Obeying God and following Him as the Spirit leads challenges you to trust Him every moment of your life. With that kind of belief, you'll share His world-changing message.

Day 272

Isaiah 47:1–49:13; Galatians 3:19–29;
Proverbs 3:27–35

*"I made known the things that would happen
long ago. From My mouth My words went
out. Then all at once I did what I said
I would, and they came to pass."*

ISAIAH 48:3

Lord, how often do we overextend ourselves? We try to be everything for everybody and wind up disappointing others, as well as ourselves and You. Lord, help us to be careful what we promise. Help us to be dependable. Let us accomplish our tasks to the best of our abilities and demonstrate a job well done.

Day 273

Isaiah 49:14–51:23; Galatians 4:1–11;
Proverbs 4:1–19

Get wisdom. Though it cost all you have, get understanding.

PROVERBS 4:7 NIV

Have you ever thought of yourself as wise? The Bible says you can be. You don't need a lot of education or a certain IQ. Real wisdom is found in God. Simply obey your Lord's commandments and make knowing Him well your first priority. Seek after wisdom, and you will find it in Him. As you daily search for truth in the Word, your understanding grows.

Day 274

Isaiah 52–54; Galatians 4:12–31;
Proverbs 4:20–27

*Thy Maker is thine husband;
the Lord of hosts is his name.*

Isaiah 54:5 kjv

Some women are single by their own choice or as part of God's plan for their lives. Others may be divorced or widowed. If you are single, you are in a highly favored position. The Lord says that He is the One who will provide for you and defend you. You can look to Him for love and companionship. He's more faithful and wise than any human husband.

Day 275

Isaiah 55–57; Galatians 5; Proverbs 5:1-14

"You will go out with joy, and be led out in peace. The mountains and the hills will break out into sounds of joy before you. And all the trees of the field will clap their hands."

ISAIAH 55:12

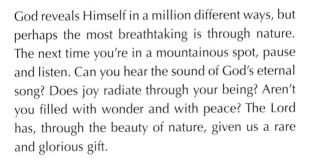

God reveals Himself in a million different ways, but perhaps the most breathtaking is through nature. The next time you're in a mountainous spot, pause and listen. Can you hear the sound of God's eternal song? Does joy radiate through your being? Aren't you filled with wonder and with peace? The Lord has, through the beauty of nature, given us a rare and glorious gift.

Day 276

Isaiah 58–59; Galatians 6; Proverbs 5:15–23

Share each other's burdens, and in this way obey the law of Christ.

GALATIANS 6:2 NLT

Have you seen the size of kids' backpacks lately? Their backs sway with the weight of books, papers, and "stuff." Kids carry these packs all day on tired shoulders. The burdens you carry around each day may be causing your shoulders to droop as well. Take those worries and burdens to God. He has promised to lighten your load by adding His shoulder to yours.

Day 277

Isaiah 60–62; Ephesians 1; Proverbs 6:1–5

Even before the world was made,
God chose us for Himself because of
His love. He planned that we should be
holy and without blame as He sees us.

EPHESIANS 1:4

You may never receive full acceptance and approval of the people in your life. But God has already given you His approval, His acceptance. Think about that. Almighty God chose you! The Bible says He created you and pronounced His work "good." He's proud of the "you" He's made, and He is moved with love for you—just as you are.

Day 278

Isaiah 63:1–65:16; Ephesians 2; Proverbs 6:6–19

*"I will comfort you as one is
comforted by his mother."*

Isaiah 66:13

Like a tender mother, God comforts His people.
When life challenges us, we have a place to renew
our faith. Instead of questioning God's compassion
because we face a trial, we can draw ever nearer
to Him, seeking to do His will. Surrounded by His
tender arms, we gain strength to go out and face the
world again.

Day 279

Isaiah 65:17–66:24; Ephesians 3:1–4:16;
Proverbs 6:20–26

---

*We will speak the truth in love, growing in
every way more and more like Christ.*

EPHESIANS 4:15 NLT

A white lie may sometimes seem more easily swallowed than the blunt truth of a situation, but God has blessed you with the help of His Holy Spirit to bring truth into the lives of others. He knows their hearts and the words that should be spoken to bring them closer to God and to you.

Day 280

Jeremiah 1–2; Ephesians 4:17–32;
Proverbs 6:27–35

*If you are angry, do not let it become sin.
Get over your anger before the day is finished.*

EPHESIANS 4:26

We have valid reasons for anger when we see wrongdoing against the innocent. But God tells us not to let that anger last long. We need to come to Him in prayer, consider the issue in Him, and ultimately leave it in His hands. Let anger push us to do good, not ruin our emotional health.

Day 281

Jeremiah 3:1–4:22; Ephesians 5; Proverbs 7:1–5

---

*Tell of your joy to each other by singing
the Songs of David and church songs.
Sing in your heart to the Lord.*

EPHESIANS 5:19

Want to try a fun experiment? The next time someone asks you how you're doing, instead of responding, "Okay," why not get more specific? Try "I'm blessed!" or "Having an awesome day!" Encourage yourself in the Lord, and He will keep those spirits lifted. And encourage one another with words of blessing as well.

Day 282

Jeremiah 4:23–5:31; Ephesians 6;
Proverbs 7:6–27

Put on the whole armour of God, that ye may be able to stand against the wiles of the devil.

EPHESIANS 6:11 KJV

Every woman should take a basic class in self-defense to protect herself in this predator-filled world. A wise woman will learn how to defend herself spiritually as well. God has provided you with a full suit of armor for that purpose—truth, righteousness, peace, faith, and salvation. Wear them everywhere you go. You have an enemy, and he wants to take all you have. Be prepared to resist and defeat him.

Day 283

Jeremiah 6:1–7:26; Philippians 1:1–26;
Proverbs 8:1–11

---

*And this is my prayer: I pray that your love will
grow more and more. I pray that you will have
better understanding and be wise in all things.*

PHILIPPIANS 1:9

The Spirit of God transforms you into His image,
but you must do your part too. You must relinquish
sin, build up your spirit by reading God's Word,
open your heart to wisdom and counsel, and
surrender your old nature to be replaced by your
new one. Your spiritual growth is intended to be a
collaboration between you and God. The work is
often difficult, but it brings great rewards.

Day 284

Jeremiah 7:27–9:16; Philippians 1:27–2:18;
Proverbs 8:12–21

*Then give me true joy by thinking the
same thoughts. Keep having the same love.
Be as one in thoughts and actions.*

PHILIPPIANS 2:2

Want to know how to bring joy to God's heart? Live in unity with your Christian brothers and sisters. When we're like-minded, it pleases our heavenly Father. Are there problems to be ironed out with a Christian friend? Troubles in your church family? Let this be the day you fulfill His joy by resolving those differences. Let unity lead the way!

Day 285

Jeremiah 9:17–11:17; Philippians 2:19–30;
Proverbs 8:22–36

---

*Those who find [wisdom] find life and
receive favor from the LORD.*

PROVERBS 8:35 NIV

Are you a wise woman? That may be a difficult question to answer. Here's an easier one: Are you the kind of friend/mother/daughter/sister that others turn to for godly advice? If the answer is yes, then you've got some of the life-giving wisdom that pleases God. You can never have too much of this kind of wisdom. Spend time today seeking more of it in His Word!

Day 286

Jeremiah 11:18–13:27; Philippians 3; Proverbs 9:1–6

My eyes are on the crown. I want to win the race and get the crown of God's call from heaven through Christ Jesus.

<small>PHILIPPIANS 3:14</small>

Ever feel like the journey's too long? Like you're not making progress? Today, ask the Lord to give you joy as you make your way toward the goal. Don't fret if things aren't happening as quickly as you want them to. Keep on pressing toward the mark. Thank Him for the process, and take time to truly take "joy in the journey."

Day 287

Jeremiah 14–15; Philippians 4; Proverbs 9:7–18

---

*Let everyone see that you are considerate in all
you do. Remember, the Lord is coming soon.*

PHILIPPIANS 4:5 NLT

The Bible says that the strong woman is also gentle—
two words that might seem contradictory. But they
aren't. The strong woman chooses to deal with
others gently—because she can. She is in control
of her emotions, her words, and her actions. Anger,
hostility—both represent the easy way out. But
gentleness requires strength. God wants to see you
become a strong, gentle woman for Him.

Day 288

Jeremiah 16–17; Colossians 1:1–23;
Proverbs 10:1–5

*I pray that God's great power will make you
strong, and that you will have joy as
you wait and do not give up.*

COLOSSIANS 1:11

There aren't enough hours in the day to do a woman's work. No wonder we often feel exhausted and unhappy. The Bible says that God strengthens us, empowering us to push through and get our jobs done. Sometimes He does that by empowering us to say no when we should, rest when we should, and keep our lives balanced. Ask Him for a transfusion for your life.

Jeremiah 18:1–20:6; Colossians 1:24–2:15;
Proverbs 10:6–14

He that walketh uprightly walketh surely.

PROVERBS 10:9 KJV

Choosing to do the right thing could mean the loss of income, a broken relationship, or an embarrassing confrontation. But whatever it takes, keep your integrity. When you do what is right, you preserve your soul. You'll make mistakes—no doubt about that—but God is there to forgive you and help you stay on track in the future. When you choose integrity, you choose the Lord.

Jeremiah 20:7–22:19; Colossians 2:16–3:4;
Proverbs 10:15–26

Think about the things of heaven,
not the things of earth.
COLOSSIANS 3:2 NLT

Human beings can be hopelessly shortsighted. But the person who plans for eternity has both the present and the future in mind. When you accepted God's forgiveness, your future in heaven was sealed. But the Bible also talks about laying up treasure in heaven. Place your priorities on those things that are eternal rather than those things that are just for this world alone.

Day 291

Jeremiah 22:20–23:40; Colossians 3:5–4:1;
Proverbs 10:27–32

---

*You have now become a new person and are
always learning more about Christ.*

COLOSSIANS 3:10

Are there people you've given up on? Maybe someone you've been praying for, for years? You're convinced he or she will never come to the Lord? Today, ponder the new beginnings in your own life. Hasn't God recreated you? Won't He do the same for others? Pray for that friend or loved one to "become a new person."

Day 292

Jeremiah 24–25; Colossians 4:2–18;
Proverbs 11:1–11

---

*Speak with them in such a way they will
want to listen to you. Do not let your talk
sound foolish. Know how to give
the right answer to anyone.*

<small>COLOSSIANS 4:6</small>

Your words are a vital part of your witness. Speak to
an unbeliever ungraciously, and chances are good
that she will never forget it. But study and grow
in the Word; then speak wisely and generously to
others, and God can use your words to win them to
His kingdom. People respond well to kindness and
flavorful speech. What are your words saying today?

Day 293

Jeremiah 26–27; 1 Thessalonians 1:1–2:8;
Proverbs 11:12–21

A gracious woman retaineth honour.

PROVERBS 11:16 KJV

As you grow in God, you will demonstrate His character in your thoughts, attitude, and behavior. Through you, His goodness becomes evident to others, and their respect for you increases. This will happen not because you demand it but because it is a natural response to God's glory. For the same reason, you must respect yourself—casting down thoughts of inferiority and unworthiness. Respect God's presence and work within you.

Day 294

Jeremiah 28–29; 1 Thessalonians 2:9–3:13;
Proverbs 11:22–26

---

*How can we give God enough thanks
for you for all the joy you give us?*

1 THESSALONIANS 3:9

Think of the people God has placed in your life—
your family members, friends, coworkers, and
other loved ones. They bring such joy and happiness to your life, don't they? Now contemplate
this: What if you'd never met any of them? How
different would your life be? These folks are such
a gift! God has given them to you as a special gift.
Remember to thank Him!

Day 295

Jeremiah 30:1–31:22; 1 Thessalonians 4:1–5:11;
Proverbs 11:27–31

Let us keep our minds awake. Let us cover our chests with faith and love. Let us cover our heads with the hope of being saved.

<small>1 THESSALONIANS 5:8</small>

Self-control is the ability to control your own behavior. You alone are responsible for your choices, decisions, and actions. God has given you the Holy Spirit to help you live as you were designed to live—a productive, fulfilled life. No matter what others do or say, you have the power to do what is right. God has given you all the tools you need to come out on top.

Day 296

Jeremiah 31:23–32:35; 1 Thessalonians 5:12–28;
Proverbs 12:1–14

Pray without ceasing.
1 Thessalonians 5:17 KJV

Haven't gotten an answer to your prayer? Don't give up. There's no time limit on speaking to God about your needs. It's just that we often work on a different time schedule from God. We want an answer yesterday, while He has something better in mind for tomorrow. So keep praying. God listens to His children and gives them the best answer, not the fastest one.

Day 297

Jeremiah 32:36–34:7; 2 Thessalonians 1–2;
Proverbs 12:15–20

---

*The way of fools seems right to them,
but the wise listen to advice.*

PROVERBS 12:15 NIV

Listening to others who are wise brings us wisdom too. Before we make serious choices, we need to seek the advice of others. How can we recognize the wise ones? Those who have experience, faith, and who have made decisions that blessed their lives can pass their wisdom on to us too. Is there some wise person you need to consult now?

Day 298

Jeremiah 34:8–36:10; 2 Thessalonians 3;
Proverbs 12:21–28

---

*The man who is right with God is a teacher to
his neighbor, but the way of the sinful
leads them the wrong way.*

PROVERBS 12:26

We need friends. But there are those who will lead
us into trouble and those who will encourage us
and lift us up in our faith. Before we draw near to
others, do we consider their spiritual impact on us?
If God is our best friend, let us be cautious not to
be led astray. When we share friendship with Jesus
and our earthly friends, we are truly blessed.

Day 299

Jeremiah 36:11–38:13; 1 Timothy 1:1–17;
Proverbs 13:1–4

---

*The soul of the lazy person has strong desires
but gets nothing, but the soul of the one who
does his best gets more than he needs.*

PROVERBS 13:4

Regardless of whether your work is in an office or in your home, each morning, you've got a job to do. God is pleased when you apply yourself diligently to the task He's given you. It may be pleasant work—it may not. Think of it as your gift to your heavenly Father for the day. Do it as if He were watching your every step—because He is.

Day 300

Jeremiah 38:14–40:6; 1 Timothy 1:18–3:13;
Proverbs 13:5–13

When the desire cometh, it is a tree of life.
PROVERBS 13:12 KJV

You are a fortunate woman! You live in a time when women can accomplish nearly anything. Are there still obstacles? Of course, but nothing you can't deal with. God has given you something special to do in this world. Ask God to guide you, lending you His wisdom, grace, and strength. Then go for it. Nothing can compare with the joy of accomplishing God's will for your life.

Day 301

Jeremiah 40:7–42:22; 1 Timothy 3:14–4:10;
Proverbs 13:14–21

*Growing strong in body is all right but
growing in God-like living is more important.
It will not only help you in this life
now but in the next life also.*

1 TIMOTHY 4:8

Do you have Dumbo flaps? You know, those fleshy
wings that hang on the underside of your arms when
you raise them. A stiff wind could create liftoff. They
say regular workouts will tighten those puppies up.
Just as we exercise muscles to make them strong, we
keep our faith in shape by exercising it. Discipline is
the way to conquer flab—physically *and* spiritually!

Day 302

Jeremiah 43–44; 1 Timothy 4:11–5:16;
Proverbs 13:22–25

---

*Show other Christians how to live by your
life. . . . Show them how to live in faith
and in love and in holy living.*

1 TIMOTHY 4:12

Setting an example for others can seem like a heavy weight—always having to watch your words and your actions. But the only way you can live worthy to represent God is to let Him live through you. Soon you will find yourself demonstrating for others that it's possible to live a pure and godly life.

Day 303

Jeremiah 45–47; 1 Timothy 5:17–6:21;
Proverbs 14:1–6

---

*A God-like life gives us much when we
are happy for what we have.*

1 TIMOTHY 6:6

Lord, so often I feel amiss. Nothing is wrong, yet I stumble around looking for something to make me feel complete. I have so much: a family's love, Your love. My best days are when I'm close to You and know I have everything I need through You.

Day 304

Jeremiah 48:1–49:6; 2 Timothy 1;
Proverbs 14:7–22

---

*He that despiseth his neighbour sinneth:
but he that hath mercy on the
poor, happy is he.*

PROVERBS 14:21 KJV

Our loving heavenly Father is so merciful toward us, and He expects us to treat others with mercy too. Did you realize that giving to those who are less fortunate than you can actually make you happy? It's true! Reach out to someone today—and watch the joy start to flow!

Day 305

Jeremiah 49:7–50:16; 2 Timothy 2;
Proverbs 14:23–27

---

*There is strong trust in the fear of the Lord,
and His children will have a safe place.*

PROVERBS 14:26

There is only one right kind of fear—the fear of God. Not that we need to cower before Him, but we must respect and honor Him and His infinite power. Those who love Him also rightly fear Him. But those who fear God need fear nothing else. He is their Refuge, the Protector whom nothing can bypass. Fear God, and you are safe.

Day 306

Jeremiah 50:17–51:14; 2 Timothy 3;
Proverbs 14:28–35

---

*All the Holy Writings are God-given and are
made alive by Him. . . . It shows [us]
how to be right with God.*

2 TIMOTHY 3:16

Did you realize that God prepares you to do good works every day of your life? How do you start? By reading the scriptures, His guidebook. There you will learn what to believe, how to act, and how to speak with love. Soon you'll be ready to put into action all you've learned.

Day 307

Jeremiah 51:15–64; 2 Timothy 4; Proverbs 15:1–9

A soft answer turneth away wrath:
but grievous words stir up anger.

PROVERBS 15:1 KJV

How you speak can strongly affect those around you.
If someone is blazing mad, do you quell that anger
with calming words or inflame it with harsh ones? Do
you start a forest fire with your sister who irritates you
or quench the blaze with soft words? Anger makes
wise decision-making impossible. But God's Word
offers advice that brings peace to our lives. Gentle
speech leads to wiser choices.

Day 308

Jeremiah 52–Lamentations 1; Titus 1:1–9;
Proverbs 15:10–17

A glad heart makes a happy face.
PROVERBS 15:13 NLT

Happiness is elusive. Because it's an emotion—like sadness and anger—it comes and goes with the circumstances. Joy is different. It's the permanent condition of the heart that is right with God. Joy isn't based on circumstances but rather the known outcome—eternity with God. Forget about the pursuit of happiness and embrace joy. It will not fail you even in your darkest days and most trying hours. Rejoice!

Day 309

Lamentations 2:1–3:38; Titus 1:10–2:15;
Proverbs 15:18–26

---

*It is because of the Lord's loving-kindness that
we are not destroyed for His loving-pity
never ends. It is new every morning.
He is so very faithful.*

LAMENTATIONS 3:22–23

Don't you love the newness of morning? The dew
on the grass? The awakening of the sun? The quiet
stillness of the day? Oh, what joy rises in our souls
as we realize that God's love and mercy are new
every morning! Each day is a fresh start, a new
chance. Grace washes over us afresh, like the
morning dew. Great is His faithfulness!

Day 310

Lamentations 3:39–5:22; Titus 3;
Proverbs 15:27–33

---

*[God saved us] from the punishment of sin.
It was not because we worked to be right
with God. It was because of His loving-
kindness that He washed our sins away.
At the same time He gave us new life
when the Holy Spirit came into our lives.*

TITUS 3:5

Could we save ourselves? No way! Even our best
efforts fall far short of God's perfection. If God had
left us on our own, we'd be eternally separated from
Him. But graciously, the Father reached down to us
through His Son, sacrificing Jesus on the cross. Then
the Spirit touched our lives in rebirth and renewal.
Together, the three Persons of the Godhead saved
us in merciful love.

Day 311

Ezekiel 1:1–3:21; Philemon; Proverbs 16:1–9

*Your love has given me great joy
and encouragement.*

Philemon 7 niv

Have you ever found yourself in need of consolation? Ever longed for someone to wrap their arms of love around you and make everything all right? God *is* that Someone. We can take great consolation in His love, which is unchanging, everlasting, and abounding. Doesn't it bring joy to your heart to see how wide, how deep, and how long the Father's love is for His children?

Day 312

Ezekiel 3:22–5:17; Hebrews 1:1–2:4;
Proverbs 16:10–21

*He who listens to the Word will find good,
and happy is he who trusts in the Lord.*
PROVERBS 16:20

Want the key to true happiness? Try wisdom. When others around you are losing their heads, losing their cool, and losing sleep over their decisions, choose to react differently. Step up to the plate. Handle matters wisely. Wise choices always lead to joyous outcomes. And along the way, you will be setting an example for others around you to follow. So, c'mon. . .get happy! Get wisdom!

Day 313

Ezekiel 6–7; Hebrews 2:5–18; Proverbs 16:22–33

*He that is slow to anger
is better than the mighty.*

PROVERBS 16:32 KJV

Our modern world does not encourage patience. Internet providers tout newer, faster technologies. What used to take days can now be done in minutes. Not everything can be rushed, though. God still does things in His own way and timing. When you feel impatient waiting for God to move on your behalf, resolve to trust Him. Surrender yourself to Him. You can be sure that He knows best.

Day 314

A dry piece of food with peace and quiet is better than a house full of food with fighting.

PROVERBS 17:1

You probably know the unsettled feeling that results from being in a fight with someone you love. Whether it's with a spouse, a parent, a sibling, or a child, misunderstandings sometimes happen and feelings can get hurt. God calls us to be the calming factor during these times of discord, reintroducing peace back into the home. Are there any fights in your life you need to work on?

Day 315

Ezekiel 11–12; Hebrews 4:4–5:10;
Proverbs 17:6–12

---

*Let us go with complete trust to the throne of
God. We will receive His loving-kindness
and have His loving-favor to help
us whenever we need it.*

HEBREWS 4:16

Don't feel shy about approaching Jesus with all
your cares. As God's child, you have a special
place in His heart. When you have failed, you
need not fear coming to the King of kings for mercy
and grace. He is just waiting for you to admit the
problem and ask for help. Seek Jesus' aid, whatever
your trouble. That's what He wants you to do.

Day 316

Ezekiel 13–14; Hebrews 5:11–6:20;
Proverbs 17:13–22

A friend loveth at all times,
and a brother is born for adversity.

PROVERBS 17:17 KJV

Tough times reveal real friends. Partly that is true because real friends are the ones who stick around when things are troublesome and uncomfortable and not at all fun. But also it is true because when you are at your worst or weakest, you can only bear to be witnessed by real friends—those who already know you inside and out and accept you just the way you are. Ask God to give you that kind of friend.

Day 317

Ezekiel 15:1–16:43; Hebrews 7;
Proverbs 17:23–28

---

*The Law of Moses could not make men right
with God. Now there is a better hope through
which we can come near to God.*

HEBREWS 7:19

Following Old Testament law used to be considered the way to achieve righteousness. But obeying rules just doesn't work for fallible humans. We fail miserably. Then Jesus came and provided a better way. He bridged the gap by offering us a personal relationship rather than rules. We get to *know* our Papa God through our personal relationship with Him.

Day 318

Ezekiel 16:44–17:24; Hebrews 8:1–9:10;
Proverbs 18:1–7

*"I have forgiven you for all that you
have done," says the Lord God.*

Ezekiel 16:63

You are forgiven. No matter what you've done. The moment you acknowledge your sin and ask to be forgiven, it's done. Strangely, that may be difficult for you to accept. You may feel you must make your own atonement. But it's a feat you will never accomplish. Only God's perfect Son was able to do the job. Abandon your pride and receive His forgiveness. Don't wait another moment.

Day 319

Ezekiel 18–19; Hebrews 9:11–28;
Proverbs 18:8–17

---

*The Law says that almost everything is made
clean by blood. Sins are not forgiven
unless blood is given.*

HEBREWS 9:22

Many people would like cheap forgiveness. They want someone to say they are okay, but they don't want to pay any price for their wrongdoing. That's not what the scriptures say. Remission of sins comes at a high price—sacrificial blood, the blood of Jesus. Jesus says you are worth this expense, and you are clean in Him. Put sin away and rejoice in His deep love for you.

Day 320

Ezekiel 20; Hebrews 10:1–25; Proverbs 18:18–24

Let us hold on to the hope we say we have and not be changed. We can trust God that He will do what He promised.

Hebrews 10:23

People sometimes break promises, but God is faithful. The promises He's made, He'll keep. You don't always know how and when, and sometimes life can mislead you into thinking your hope is lost. But if you are determined to hold on, your course will become clear. God's counting on you to stay the course and never give up.

Day 321

Ezekiel 21–22; Hebrews 10:26–39;
Proverbs 19:1–8

You must be willing to wait without giving up. After you have done what God wants you to do, God will give you what He promised you.

HEBREWS 10:36

The dictionary defines *perseverance* as "a quest to complete an idea, purpose, or task despite obstacles." Father, help us to run toward the fruit of the Spirit. The ideas, purposes, tasks there seem so appealing, yet because we are human, we often get sidetracked by temptation. Help us to strive after You.

Day 322

Ezekiel 23; Hebrews 11:1–31; Proverbs 19:9–14

And it is impossible to please God without faith. Anyone who wants to come to him must believe that God exists and that he rewards those who sincerely seek him.

HEBREWS 11:6 NLT

Belief is one of those things you can't see with your eyes, but you still have it. You believe a chair will hold you when you sit in it. You can't explain the physics of it, but you sit. Belief in God is like that. You put your trust in Him that He will do what He said He would do. His Word is filled with those promises.

Day 323

Ezekiel 24–26; Hebrews 11:32–40;
Proverbs 19:15–21

---

*Many are the plans in a person's heart,
but it is the Lord's purpose that prevails.*

PROVERBS 19:21 NIV

Most of us have countless plans and dreams in our hearts—a dream home, an ideal career, the perfect husband, and adorable children—the list is endless. We can plot and scheme the future on our own terms. Or we can guess at what God wants for us. The third and best way is to seek God's plans first—then follow.

Day 324

Ezekiel 27–28; Hebrews 12:1–13;
Proverbs 19:22–29

*Let us keep looking to Jesus. Our faith
comes from Him and He is the One
Who makes it perfect.*

HEBREWS 12:2

God is writing a story of faith through your life. What will it describe? Will it be a chronicle of challenges overcome, like the Old Testament story of Joseph? Or a near tragedy turned into joy, like that of the prodigal son? Whatever your account says, if you love Jesus, the end is never in question. Those who love Him finish in heaven despite their trials on earth. The long, weary path ends in His arms. Today, write a chapter in your faithful narrative of God's love.

Day 325

Ezekiel 29–30; Hebrews 12:14–29;
Proverbs 20:1–18

Even a child is known by his doings,
whether his work be pure,
and whether it be right.

PROVERBS 20:11 KJV

What do your actions say about you? Sure, you can profess to be a Christian, to believe in the Bible, to have a relationship with Jesus, but the true test of the heart shows through what you do. Before you tell others about your faith, what do they already think about you by what they've seen? As long as you have breath in your lungs, it's not too late to choose the path of righteousness.

Day 326

Ezekiel 31–32; Hebrews 13; Proverbs 20:19–24

Don't forget to do good and to share with those in need. These are the sacrifices that please God.

HEBREWS 13:16 NLT

The true meaning of hospitality is opening up your heart to others, making them feel at home in your presence. It doesn't require a fancy house or a gourmet meal. When you reach out to someone else with love and acceptance, you have shown that person hospitality. Look around you. Ask God to show you those people whom you can minister to just by opening your heart.

Day 327

Ezekiel 33:1–34:10; James 1; Proverbs 20:25–30

My Christian brothers, you should be happy when you have all kinds of tests.

JAMES 1:2

Joy? To be faced with tests should cause us joy? Hard to imagine, isn't it? But God calls us to joy when our situation is difficult. It is a joy to Him that we have stood firm in faith, and He calls us to share His delight. That doesn't mean we seek out trials but that we face the situation hand in hand with God. In trials, our spiritual strength increases.

Day 328

Ezekiel 34:11–36:15; James 2; Proverbs 21:1–8

"I will bring good to them and to the places around My hill. I will give them rain when they need it."

EZEKIEL 34:26

How do we shift from one phase of life to the next? We can move forward with joy leading the way when we realize that God is the giver of the seasons. He designed them and showers us with blessings as we move through each one, even the tough ones! Good news! Change is always just around the bend. Oh, the joy of knowing the hard times won't last.

Day 329

Ezekiel 36:16–37:28; James 3; Proverbs 21:9–18

A new heart also will I give you,
and a new spirit will I put within you.

EZEKIEL 36:26 KJV

Some of the most surprising news about God's presence is that He does more than fix you up the best He can—somehow He makes you brand new. He doesn't delete the consequences that still have to be battled through—but He does have the power to change your heart and help you manage those consequences. Ask Him to make you new!

Day 330

Ezekiel 38–39; James 4:1–5:6; Proverbs 21:19–24

Anyone who chooses to be a friend of the world becomes an enemy of God.

JAMES 4:4 NIV

When Christ becomes your best friend, other relationships may become distant. Old carnal friendships no longer seem so attractive. Your lifestyles clash, and old friends become confused. But this separation is part of God's plan of holiness. Jesus disconnects you from the world and draws you close to His people—Christian friends who share your love for Him. Together, you may reach out to those old friends for Jesus too.

Day 331

Ezekiel 40; James 5:7–20; Proverbs 21:25–31

The prayer given in faith will heal the sick man, and the Lord will raise him up.

JAMES 5:15

Have you ever wondered why God instructed church leaders to pray for the sick? Perhaps it's because when we're sick, we often don't have the strength to pray for ourselves. We need our brothers and sisters in the Lord to cry out on our behalf. If you're struggling with illness, call for your Christian friends or church leaders to come and pray with you. What joy. . .when healing comes!

Day 332

Ezekiel 41:1–43:12; 1 Peter 1:1–12;
Proverbs 22:1–9

*May God give you more and
more grace and peace.*

1 Peter 1:2 nlt

As you see God's blessings in your life, look inward
as well. God has also provided you with an abun-
dance of grace and peace. Women are wonderfully
emotional people, the keepers of the inner life. If
your inner places are dark and empty, invite God to
fill them to overflowing with His goodness.

Day 333

Ezekiel 43:13–44:31; 1 Peter 1:13–2:3;
Proverbs 22:10–23

Get your minds ready for good use. Keep awake. Set your hope now and forever on the loving-favor to be given you when Jesus Christ comes again.

1 PETER 1:13

There are moments in every woman's life when her emotions take over. When those times come, God wants you to walk by faith and not by sight—being led by confidence in Him rather than your feelings. The gift of self-control will put you in His best light and keep you from responding foolishly. He stands ready to help you choose self-control. Believe in Him because He believes in you.

Ezekiel 45–46; 1 Peter 2:4–17;
Proverbs 22:24–29

---

*But you are a chosen group of people. You
are the King's religious leaders. You are a holy
nation. You belong to God. He has done this
for you so you can tell others how God has
called you out of darkness into His great light.*

1 PETER 2:9

Your life is a song of praise that rises to your Father. He revels in your decision to take His hand and step out of darkness into light. It's why He sent His Son, Jesus, to live and die and rise again. You are His prize, the certain reward of His great sacrifice. Each time you say yes to life, yes to eternal values, you are praising Him.

Day 335

Ezekiel 47–48; 1 Peter 2:18–3:7; Proverbs 23:1–9

Do not let your beauty come from the outside. . . . Your beauty should come from. . .the heart. This is the kind that lasts. Your beauty should be a gentle and quiet spirit. In God's sight this is of great worth and no amount of money can buy it.

1 PETER 3:3–4

Most women care how they look. That's why we carry mirrors in our purses and spend billions of dollars on makeup each year. There's nothing wrong with looking good on the outside as long as we remember to primp our inner selves too. He wants your beauty to be heart deep. Work to be as fully beautiful as you were created to be.

Day 336

Daniel 1:1–2:23; 1 Peter 3:8–4:19;
Proverbs 23:10–16

---

*Finally, all of you, be like-minded,
be sympathetic, love one another,
be compassionate and humble.*

1 PETER 3:8 NIV

The family of God is in many respects like your natural family. You love them profoundly, but very often they can make you throw up your hands in frustration. Just like you, they all have those areas where they are still growing and learning. When conflicts come, don't turn and run! It's important to work it out and see it through—for your Father's sake.

Day 337

Daniel 2:24–3:30; 1 Peter 5; Proverbs 23:17–25

Casting all your care upon him;
for he careth for you.

1 PETER 5:7 KJV

You don't have a care in the world that you cannot share with Jesus. There isn't anything He doesn't want to hear from you. Before you ask a friend to pray for you (and you should do that), be certain to share your care with Jesus. There's no worry He can't alleviate or remove.

Day 338

Daniel 4; 2 Peter 1; Proverbs 23:26–35

*Do not give up. And as you wait
and do not give up, live God-like.*

2 PETER 1:6

Like it or not, waiting is a big part of life. As children, we impatiently wait for Christmas to come. As adults, we eagerly anticipate a wedding day, the birth of a child, a job promotion, retirement. As Christians, we're awaiting Jesus' return. Waiting is always difficult, but the Father reminds us to never give up. He's coming, so be ready!

Day 339

Daniel 5; 2 Peter 2; Proverbs 24:1–18

But the Lord knows how to help men who are right with God when they are tempted.

2 PETER 2:9

Feeling surrounded by temptations? God hasn't forgotten you. He knows how to protect His children from harm and offers His wisdom to His children. Maybe you need to avoid places that could lead you into sin—that may mean taking action like finding a new job or new friends. When God is trying to protect you, don't resist. Sin is never better than knowing Him.

Day 340

Daniel 6:1–7:14; 2 Peter 3; Proverbs 24:19–27

---

*Nevertheless we, according to his promise,
look for new heavens and a new earth,
wherein dwelleth righteousness.*

2 PETER 3:13 KJV

Wars. Threats. Recessions. Assassinations. Every day the news bombards us with the shortcomings of an imperfect world. Father, every day we fall short. How grateful I am that You've promised us a better place. My eyes stay open through the watches of the night, that I may meditate on Your promises.

Day 341

Daniel 7:15–8:27; 1 John 1:1–2:17;
Proverbs 24:28–34

---

*Do not love the world or anything in
the world. If anyone loves the world,
the Father's love is not in him.*

1 JOHN 2:15

※

This verse is likely to hit us right where we live. The world's way tempts us more than we'd like to admit. But when we feel the pull of worldliness, do we remember that we're actually making a larger decision about loving God? Gaining the small, temporal things is not worth compromising our faith. Let's save our love for the One who really deserves it.

Day 342

Daniel 9–10; 1 John 2:18–29; Proverbs 25:1–12

This is what he promised us—eternal life.
1 JOHN 2:25 NIV

Ever had a friend or loved one break a promise? What about you? Ever broken a promise? We all fail in this area, don't we? Thankfully, God is not a promise breaker. When He promised you would spend eternity with Him if you accepted the work of His Son on the cross. . .He meant it. Doesn't it bring joy to your heart to know God won't break His promises?

Day 343

Daniel 11–12; 1 John 3:1–12; Proverbs 25:13–17

*See what great love the Father has for us
that He would call us His children.
And that is what we are.*

1 John 3:1

God does not give His love in dribs and drabs. He lavishes it on us when we come to Him in faith. All along, He was waiting to make us His children, and we were the ones who resisted. But once we face Him as His children, God's love lets loose in our lives. Nothing is too good for His obedient children. Praise God that He loves you that much!

Day 344

Hosea 1–3; 1 John 3:13–4:16; Proverbs 25:18–28

Dear friends, let us love each other,
because love comes from God. Those who
love are God's children and they know God.

1 JOHN 4:7

Want to see love? Look at God. Seeking love in this world is bound to be confusing. But in our Lord, we see the clarity of real love—love we can share with our families, friends, and fellow believers. Love for our enemies. Love for our Savior. Love isn't just a feeling, but the actions we take as we follow Him.

Day 345

We know God's Son has come. He has given us the understanding to know Him Who is the true God. We are joined together with the true God through His Son, Jesus Christ. He is the true God and the life that lasts forever.

1 JOHN 5:20

How do we know God? Through His Son, Jesus, who helps us understand the love of His Father. There is no space, no difference of opinion, between Father and Son. When we know the Son, we know God truly. Trust in one is trust in both.

Hosea 7–10; 2 John; Proverbs 26:17–21

Without wood a fire goes out;
without a gossip a quarrel dies down.
PROVERBS 26:20 NIV

Gossip is one of those "small" sins that creeps into Christian circles, sometimes without us knowing it. Proverbs describes gossip as a fire that spreads quickly when more gossip fuel is added. Take away the fuel and the fire stops! Be a firefighter and snuff out the destruction of gossip in your friendships today.

Day 347

Hosea 11–14; 3 John; Proverbs 26:22–27:9

*Ointment and perfume rejoice the heart:
so doth the sweetness of a man's
friend by hearty counsel.*

PROVERBS 27:9 KJV

Friendship is a wonderful gift from God. A good friend leaves behind a "pleasant scent." And when you find a friend who offers wise counsel, you are doubly blessed! Today, don't just seek to *find* a friend like that; seek to *be* a friend like that. Leave behind a pleasant aroma to those God has placed in your life.

Day 348

Joel 1:1–2:17; Jude; Proverbs 27:10–17

There is One Who can keep you from falling and can bring you before Himself free from all sin. He can give you great joy as you stand before Him in His shining-greatness.

JUDE 24

Our obedience makes God happy—and should make us happy too. In fact, the more difficult it is to obey, the more joyful we should be. Why? Because a big situation calls for a big God. And our God is bigger than anything we could ask or think. So, if you're struggling in the area of obedience, surrender your will. Enter into joyful obedience.

Day 349

Joel 2:18–3:21; Revelation 1:1–2:11;
Proverbs 27:18–27

*Be happy in the Lord your God. For He has
given the early rain to help you. He has
poured down much rain for you, both fall
and spring rains, as before.*

JOEL 2:23

As human beings, we are limited in what we can
provide for others—our resources are finite. But
God has no limits. He does more than just rain
down His blessings on us; He sends abundant
showers of blessing in every season of our lives.
You are a rich woman. Once you see all God has
provided for you, you won't ever want to come in
out of the rain.

Day 350

Amos 1:1–4:5; Revelation 2:12–29;
Proverbs 28:1–8

---

*He that hath an ear, let him hear what
the Spirit saith unto the churches.*

REVELATION 2:17 KJV

We need to "lean in" to the Lord on a daily basis.
Listen to His still, small voice. Catch a glimpse of
His vision for the church. Ride on the wind of the
Spirit. Today, as you draw close to the Lord, listen
closely. What is He speaking into your life? May
your joy be full as you "tune in" to the voice of the
Holy Spirit.

Day 351

Amos 4:6–6:14; Revelation 3; Proverbs 28:9–16

"I know what you are doing. You are not cold or hot. I wish you were one or the other. But because you are warm, and not hot or cold, I will spit you out of My mouth."

REVELATION 3:15–16

Have you ever come back from a retreat or worship session completely energized for God? The truth is that the Father wants us to be on fire for Him all the time. Being lukewarm in our faith isn't an option. God doesn't want fence riders. Dig deeper into His Word to find the spark you need to ignite the flame!

Day 352

Amos 7–9; Revelation 4:1–5:5;
Proverbs 28:17–24

*The trustworthy person will get a rich reward,
but a person who wants quick riches
will get into trouble.*

PROVERBS 28:20 NLT

We've all had tasks that looked easy at the onset, but later threatened to scuttle our resolve. We wonder if it's worth it to hang on. But when we do, we find that the reward of the task accomplished is even sweeter. Are you wondering if you can finish the task God has assigned to you? Don't give up. Your faithfulness to God's purposes holds the promise of great reward. Ask God to help you faithfully carry on until the job is done.

Day 353

Obadiah–Jonah; Revelation 5:6–14;
Proverbs 28:25–28

*"But I will give gifts in worship to You with
a thankful voice. I will give You what I have
promised. The Lord is the One Who saves."*

JONAH 2:9

Gifts wrapped in paper and bows surround us at Christmastime. What do you plan to give to the Father this year? He doesn't want the latest must-have toy or gadget. He wants your worship—every day of the year!

Day 354

Micah 1:1–4:5; Revelation 6:1–7:8;
Proverbs 29:1–8

---

*They will beat their swords into plows,
and their spears into cutting hooks. Nation will
not lift up sword against nation, and they
will never learn war any more.*

MICAH 4:3

At Christmastime we talk a lot about peace on earth. But peace isn't found in the celebration surrounding a holiday or the goodwill we feel toward each other. True peace is found only in God, who offers the true contentment and stillness of His serenity. Share your knowledge of this peace with others this holiday season!

Day 355

Micah 4:6–7:20; Revelation 7:9–8:13;
Proverbs 29:9–14

---

*Therefore I will look unto the LORD;
I will wait for the God of my
salvation: my God will hear me.*

MICAH 7:7 KJV

If there's anything more frustrating than waiting for someone who never shows, it's trying to talk to someone who isn't listening. Mothers are well acquainted with this exercise in futility, as are wives, daughters, and sisters. But the Bible tells us that God hears us when we talk to Him. He shows up when we wait for Him. He will not disappoint us.

Nahum; Revelation 9–10; Proverbs 29:15–23

Where there is no understanding of the Word of the Lord, the people do whatever they want to, but happy is he who keeps the law.

PROVERBS 29:18

Ever wish you could see into tomorrow? Wish you knew what was coming around the bend? While we can't see into the future, we can prepare for it by trusting God to bring us His very best. We can prepare for it by staying close to the Lord and spending time in His Word. Peace and joy come when we trust God with our future!

Day 357

Habakkuk; Revelation 11; Proverbs 29:24–27

*I will rejoice in the Lord, I will be
joyful in God my Savior.*

HABAKKUK 3:18 NIV

Perhaps you've been waiting on pins and needles for something to happen—a promised promotion, an amazing opportunity, something wonderful. Instead, you get bad news. Things aren't going to pan out the way you expected. What do you do now? Instead of giving in to disappointment, continue to rejoice in the Lord and watch the disappointment lift. He will replace your sorrows with great joy.

Day 358

Zephaniah; Revelation 12; Proverbs 30:1-6

"The Lord your God is with you, a Powerful One Who wins the battle. He will have much joy over you. With His love He will give you new life. He will have joy over you with loud singing."

ZEPHANIAH 3:17

It's fun to picture God celebrating over us. Can you imagine? He sings over us! He dances over us. He rejoices over us! What joy floods our souls as we realize our Father God, like a loving daddy, celebrates His love for His children. Today, reflect on the thought that God—with great joy in His voice—is singing over you.

Haggai; Revelation 13:1–14:13;
Proverbs 30:7–16

I have chosen thee, saith the LORD of hosts.

HAGGAI 2:23 KJV

Out of all of God's creation, He chose us lowly humans to share His love with us, to send His Son to us, to offer us eternity with Him. On this day that we celebrate the birth of Jesus, thank Him— worship Him, celebrate Him, give Him the honor due to His name—for choosing you.

Day 360

Zechariah 1–4; Revelation 14:14–16:3;
Proverbs 30:17–20

---

*"The things You do are great and powerful. You
are the All-powerful Lord God. You are always
right and true in everything You do.
You are King of all nations."*

REVELATION 15:3

We serve a perfect God. He's perfect in His power,
in His actions, in His will. When we accept His
perfect grace through His perfect Son, Jesus, we
align ourselves with the One who holds the future
in His hands. Praise Him today because His perfect
plan includes you!

Day 361

Zechariah 5–8; Revelation 16:4–21;
Proverbs 30:21–28

---

*"Lord God, the All-powerful One! What You
decide about people is right and true."*

REVELATION 16:7

The Father God knew you before you were a
twinkle in your mother's eye. He decided your
personality quirks, endearing qualities, and even
your temperament. The greatness of you can only
be realized with God's help. Today, allow Him to
mold you into His unique child.

Zechariah 9–11; Revelation 17:1–18:8;
Proverbs 30:29–33

---

*As for you, because of the blood of My
agreement with you, I have set your people
free from the deep hole that has no
water. Return to the strong city,
you prisoners who have hope.*

ZECHARIAH 9:11–12

In the book *The Count of Monte Cristo*, Edmond Dantes is unjustly imprisoned in the darkest of dungeons—bitter, hopeless, helpless. Against all odds, God fills him with hope and enables him to escape. Have you ever felt trapped in your hopelessness? Financial difficulties, poor health, unemployment, rocky marriage, delinquent children—there are countless dungeons that shackle us. But God promises hope and freedom from our prisons. Jesus bailed us out!

Day 363

Zechariah 12–14; Revelation 18:9–24;
Proverbs 31:1–9

*Speak up and judge fairly;
defend the rights of the poor and needy.*

PROVERBS 31:9 NIV

It's easy to become desensitized to the plight of suffering people. Whether it be the homeless, storm-ravaged coastlines, or ethnic cleansing on the other side of the world, God wants us to stand up for these people. Today, ask God how He wants you to make a difference. He may call you to prayer, financial support, or even traveling to these places to lend a hand. Are you ready to answer His call?

Day 364

Malachi 1–2; Revelation 19–20;
Proverbs 31:10–17

Who can find a good wife? For she is worth far more than rubies that make one rich.

PROVERBS 31:10

Are you a virtuous woman? If so, you are truly valuable, no matter how unbelievers criticize you. Proverbs 31 says you can have a profitable life with good relationships, a happy home life, and successful business ventures if you run your life according to God's principles. So don't worry about the opinions of others if they don't mesh with God's. Instead, obey Him and be a valuable jewel to your Lord.

Day 365

Malachi 3–4; Revelation 21–22;
Proverbs 31:18–31

*She openeth her mouth with wisdom;
and in her tongue is the law of kindness.*

PROVERBS 31:26 KJV

Have you ever known someone who epitomized wisdom? What set her apart from others? A truly wise person thinks carefully before speaking and only opens her mouth when wisdom is ready to flow out. Kindness is on her tongue. There's great joy in "becoming" wise in this way. Today, guard your tongue! Think before you speak. By doing so, you bring joy to others. . .and yourself.

Bible Encouragement
for Your Heart

Read through the Bible in a Year Devotional

This lovely devotional features a simple plan for reading through the Bible in one year with an accompanying devotional thought inspired by that day's Bible reading. Each day's devotion will encourage you to read a passage from the Old Testament, New Testament, and Psalms or Proverbs and provides a relevant spiritual takeaway for practical, everyday living.

DiCarta / 978-1-68322-756-4 / $16.99